Out of Area or Out of Reach?

European Military Support for Operations in Southwest Asia

John E. Peters
Howard Deshong

National Defense Research Institute

Prepared for the
Office of the Secretary of Defense

RAND

How suitable would the military forces of Europe—principally those of NATO but conceivably others as well—be for a contingency operation in Southwest Asia in the next five or ten years? Attempting to answer this question provides insights into a host of important issues: the state of European forces, their preparedness for operations in a remote, austere, harsh, and militarily demanding theater of operations, and their ability to form a "coalition of the willing" to share the burden of defending a vital resource, the region's oil. Moreover, the process of answering the question offers an opportunity to contemplate how regional actors might respond to an incursion from the West: how they might resist, what means they might employ, and what strategy they might follow.

Focusing on the European contribution to a coalition provides a useful test of European military prowess. It identifies the capabilities and resources that the United States might advocate for its allies to round out a European contingent to Southwest Asia.

Iraq's defeat at the hands of the U.S.-led coalition in Operation Desert Storm made a deep impression on other anti-status-quo states in the region, including Iran and Syria. It is therefore worthwhile to examine what their options might be for opposing a Western contingency force. They might adopt a conventional military defense or try an approach that avoids Western strengths in conventional operations. This analysis does not make predictions on how an adversary might react or attempt to determine what specific strategies a given regime prefers (that task lies with the intelligence community), but seeks only to identify the relative advantages and disadvantages of various approaches.

Nor does the study forecast when certain actors will have specific military capabilities. The analysis is predicated upon the notion that nuclear and biological weapons, missiles, and high-quality conventional arms will appear in the arsenals of anti-status-quo states in the near term and are therefore worth thinking about. Indeed, the arms race is already under way. Where estimates of static force measures appear, their purpose is to pose one kind of credible military capability that might confront the Western contingency force at some point in the near future.

This report represents an initial examination of the issues described above. The effort was undertaken as part of a project for the Office of the Under Secretary of Defense for Policy entitled "West European Military Contributions to Persian Gulf Security and Related Missions." Research was conducted in the International Security and Defense Policy Center within RAND's National Defense Research Institute (NDRI). NDRI is a federally funded research and development center sponsored by the Office of the Secretary of Defense, the Joint Staff, and the defense agencies. The material presented here is intended to be helpful to U.S. government officials who deal with defense policy, Alliance planning, military strategy, and force development. It will also be of interest to other analysts following these issues. In general, this report should inform the ongoing discussion of U.S.-European cooperation for out-of-area missions.

CONTENTS

FIGURES

TABLES

The Southwest Asia envisioned in this study is a very dangerous place in which many actors have amassed substantial modern military arsenals. Non-status-quo states can intimidate their moderate neighbors into passivity, denying a Western expedition regional support and use of local facilities through political activity or threats of nuclear and biological reprisals. Potential adversaries in the region field capable military forces—perhaps as many as eight divisions—that have mitigated their shortcomings in training and logistics through asymmetrical strategies that avoid the Western advantage in a conventional, force-to-force engagement. Moreover, some of these potential adversaries can appeal to large, sympathetic Islamic populations living in Europe, posing a threat of terrorism and other activities in the event that Europeans intrude into Southwest Asia.

Any European expeditionary force intended for missions beyond the periphery of the continent is hobbled somewhat by the fact that the security architecture in Europe that would make collective action possible is still developing and somewhat inchoate. Many European nations continue to conceive of their security in terms that focus on more-immediate threats to their territory. Most envision out-of-area operations as involving modest crisis-response activities near their own frontiers, such as the current activities in the Balkans. As a result, only a small portion of each country's military is organized for out-of-area operations, and none of the states has developed the long-range transportation, rotation base, or logistic infrastructure to sustain a protracted mission in a distant, austere, and harsh theater against a resolute opponent threatening open warfare.

Two candidate organizations for multilateral military action are the ACE Rapid Reaction Corps (ARRC) and the Eurocorps. Unilateral action is all but out of the question, since the West Europeans have organized themselves in multinational formations to avoid the dangers they perceive in "renationalization" of defense. Both of these multinational corps are works in progress and thus are difficult to assess completely, since some of their capabilities have not yet been fully developed. Both corps manifest serious deficiencies in long-range transportation and neither formation is nearly as capable as an equivalent U.S. corps. Neither corps is able to project significant military power into Southwest Asia or sustain a long-term presence there. That said, these units may represent a high water mark for European military capability, since there seems to be no political basis that would support a more robust expeditionary force.

Ultimately, lack of regional support, the confluence of limited capability to project significant military power, political reluctance to engage a determined adversary far from Europe, and fear of the domestic consequences of launching an operation in Southwest Asia may produce multinational military paralysis. Nevertheless, the Europeans could pursue several paths to improve their ability for expeditionary operations. In some instances, they need only reorganize current military assets for more effective employment. In other cases, they must reach a new consensus on the role of NATO and other regional organizations, and the degree to which such organizations' personnel, facilities, and other assets would or would not be available to support coalitions of the willing. In still other instances, the Europeans must first agree that their vital interests are sufficiently threatened by influences beyond their immediate frontiers to warrant spending for additional military capabilities.

The Europeans should organize their existing assault shipping, carriers, and transports to support multinational deployments. The older, less capable large-deck carriers might be converted to CVHs or LPHs to support amphibious operations. Next, the Europeans should be encouraged to update and expand their air fleets. The United States should promote the notion that old airframes should be replaced no less than one-for-one with new, more-capable aircraft. In addition, the Europeans would benefit from more tankers to extend the reach of their air transports.

Since coalitions of the willing seem to be the principal basis for collective military action, each of the European nations should be encouraged to create a strategic command, control, and communications brigade or battalion that will enable its forces to maintain contact with its national leadership, direct its own subordinates, and integrate into the communications networks of the ARRC, the Eurocorps, or other *ad hoc* formations.

Any expedition venturing abroad will need missile and air defenses. The countries currently contemplating participation in the Corps SAM air defense program should be encouraged to do so.

If the Europeans can agree on the future role of NATO and other regional organizations, the following measures would be useful. The Alliance's Major NATO Commands (MNCs) lack organic capabilities and cannot contract for commercial support if deployed abroad. NATO should build the political authority and contracting procedures to do so. The Alliance should acquire and train a multinational battle staff that is prepared to direct complex operations. Most important, the Alliance must update its consultative and decisionmaking procedures to enable it to respond promptly to rapidly developing events.

To the degree that European nations determine that they must be prepared to protect vital interests beyond their borders and that doing so warrants increased defense spending, two initiatives would be prudent. First, any sizable contingency force requires echelons-above-corps units to sustain it in long-term operations. The allies should therefore be encouraged to develop their force structure above the corps and to create a theater army support command that could provide the necessary services and support. Second, one of the major features that distinguishes the European expeditionary capability described here from that of U.S. forces is the absence of maritime prepositioned squadrons. Even a modest squadron of four ships could make a substantial difference.

More daunting than the difficulties involved in reorganizing the available military resources for an expedition, however, is the matter of generating collective political resolve for concerted military action. An operational paralysis pervades European security. Until an effective European security regime emerges that can provide guidelines and mechanisms for collective military action to be held in common, Europe will remain incapable of prompt and unified military intervention or crisis response.

In addition to the measures noted above, the United States should exert its leadership to resolve the prevailing strategic paralysis in Europe, help to craft a new consensus on collective military activity, and demonstrate to its European partners that prompt, resolute action can protect mutual interests well beyond the borders of Europe from hostile influences. At a minimum, the United States should do the following:

- Use military-to-military contacts among Partnership for Peace (PFP) states to promote a common lexicon of military terms and an agreed set of operational practices that would support interoperability.

- Hold bilateral staff talks with interested states to establish what near-term support their forces would require from the United States to participate in a combined expeditionary force.

- Seek to establish a timetable and force goals with interested states to promote coordinated force development.

- Include in the joint five-year exercise schedule combined activities that would require participating European states to plan and execute a brigade-sized deployment using U.S. long-range transportation.

- In instances where a European state is interested in obtaining planning assistance, deploy a U.S. joint planning cell to the ministry of defense or appropriate armed forces headquarters to assist in organizing and planning for deployment of the state's expeditionary forces.

ACKNOWLEDGMENTS

Long-time friend and colleague Kurt B. Reineke was kind enough to review selected portions of the manuscript and to offer suggestions that improved it considerably. The report has also benefited significantly from reviews and comments by colleagues Milton G. Weiner and Robert Howe, and from a discussion with David Gompert. Any errors, of course, are the authors' alone.

GLOSSARY

ACE	Allied Command Europe
ACV	Armored combat vehicle
AEW	Airborne early warning
AFCENT	Allied Forces, Center
AFSOUTH	Allied Forces, South
AIFV	Armored infantry fighting vehicle
APC	Armored personnel carrier
ARM	Anti-radar missile
ARRC	ACE Rapid Reaction Corps
ATGM	Anti-tank guided missile
AWACS	Airborne warning and control system
CENTCOM	Central Command
CFE	Conventional Forces in Europe (treaty)
CIA	Central Intelligence Agency
Corps SAM	A new air defense program
CSCE	Conference on Security and Cooperation in Europe
CVH	Aircraft carrier, helicopter
FAR	*Force d'Action Rapide*
FLA	Future large aircraft
GPS	Global Positioning System
kT	Kiloton
KTO	Kuwaiti Theater of Operations
LANDSAT	Commercial earth surveillance satellite
LGB	Laser-guided bomb

LPD	Landing platform, dock
LPH	Landing platform, helicopter
LSD	Landing ship, dock
LST	Landing ship, tank
MCMV	Mine countermeasure vessel
MLRS	Multiple Launch Rocket System
MNC	Major NATO Command
NACC	North Atlantic Cooperation Council
NATO	North Atlantic Treaty Organization
NBC	Nuclear, biological, chemical
OOTW	Operations other than war
PFP	Partnership for Peace
Pk	Probability of kill
Ro-Ro	Roll-on, roll-off
SAM	Surface-to-air missile
SSM	Surface-to-surface missile
TBD	To be determined
TOGS	Thermal and optical gunsight
TOW	Wire guided, optically tracked (missile)
UN	United Nations
USNI	U.S. Naval Institute
WEU	Western European Union
⊠	Infantry unit

Chapter One

INTRODUCTION

Most of the European military establishments have been in decline since the end of the Cold War. The European members of NATO have all undergone comprehensive defense reviews and many have sustained major reductions. Of the 14 European members of the Atlantic Alliance, only France pursues a defense plan that includes increased spending in real terms and a net gain in military capability.[1] Yet, while the Europeans reduce their forces, they continue to develop a European security architecture that they hope will provide for effective collective action, rationalize their military capabilities, and prevent the renationalization of defense. At present, the security architecture is more apt to create strategic paralysis and confusion than coordinated military effort, but the Europeans nevertheless pursue a program that will extend security eastward and equip their forces to act together in defense of European interests. Thus far, they have reorganized NATO for crisis response and made limited progress in harmonizing the roles of the Western European Union (WEU) and NATO. The North Atlantic Cooperation Council (NACC) and the Partnership for Peace (PFP) have made the first efforts to extend security and military cooperation to the countries of Central Europe. A significant number of European nations have supported peace operations in the Balkans and elsewhere.

Europe, and especially the members of NATO, have invested an enormous effort in redesigning their military capabilities for the fu-

---

[1] See Admiral Jacques Lanxade, "French Defense Policy after the White Paper," *RUSI Journal,* April 1994, pp. 17–21.

ture. It is therefore a fair question to ask how they are doing. What is their net capability to defend a major European interest? Assessments of European performance in Bosnia and similar operations would yield only incomplete answers because the allies are not conducting ground combat operations there and because the area of operations lies within Europe, relatively close at hand. This study attempts a more complete answer by first evaluating European performance in Desert Storm and second by examining Europe's ability to operate in the Southwest Asia of the near future. While any European operation in Southwest Asia would in all likelihood be conducted in conjunction with a U.S. effort, and while any robust European military action may be highly contingent upon U.S. leadership, this study downplays the U.S. role to focus exclusively on the European contribution.

The Gulf War and future Southwest Asia cases seem appropriate gauges of Europe's military prowess for several reasons. The Gulf War involved some of NATO's most-capable forces—those of France, Italy, and the United Kingdom. If those forces experienced certain shortcomings and operational problems, it may be that less-capable allies would as well. An examination of the Gulf War performance can therefore be used, at least within limits, as a rough assessment of current European capabilities. Of course, the Europeans did not fight the Gulf War alone; they enjoyed U.S. support of all kinds. In addition to its political-military leadership, the United States provided most of the combat forces as well—75 percent of coalition air and 60 percent of ground forces. Furthermore, recent force reductions and reorganizations may have destroyed capabilities that were important in the Gulf War. In some instances, the various military establishments, especially France's, have corrected shortcomings identified in the conflict.

However, because Europe continues its heavy dependence upon the region's oil, is important to understand what the Europeans could contribute toward the defense of this resource. Southwest Asia is, after all, a very demanding arena for military operations. It is austere and distant from Europe, severely tasking transport and logistics. The climate and terrain are harsh, thus testing equipment and troops. The countries of the area pursue military modernization and rearmament programs that produce formidable armories of modern weapons, rivaling Europe's own arsenal. Finally, Southwest Asia is riven with suspicion, hostility, and claims and counterclaims that jeopardize access to oil.

This report takes a simple approach. It examines the Gulf War experience to determine in what areas the allies lacked equipment or capabilities. It then contemplates possible military advances, plans, and developments in Southwest Asia and Europe in order to sketch the dimensions of a notional regional security environment and some sense of what kind of threat might confront a European expeditionary force. The study draws on individual European national statements of future defense plans, annual force declarations mandated by the Conventional Forces in Europe (CFE) treaty, commercial data bases, and similar unclassified sources of information. Estimates of Southwest Asian states' military capabilities result from synthesizing information from commercial data bases, academic strategic surveys, and scholarly journals. Unlike the process of drafting a National Intelligence Estimate, however, the point is not to forecast specifics, but to anticipate the types of developments that would have the greatest implications for European intervention. Thus, the study downplays the activities of moderate states that might ameliorate a crisis in the region. Once the military outlines of the theater emerge, the report examines Europe's ability to operate successfully in such conditions. Drawing from an examination of the Gulf War, the study assesses how wide the gaps between capabilities and requirements might be. The identification and measurement of these gaps provides U.S. defense officials with some notion of the resources that the Europeans might ask the United States to provide to support their operations.

Chapter Two

EUROPEAN FORCES IN DESERT STORM

Some of the most-capable European forces participated in the Gulf War. An examination of their performance during Operations Desert Shield and Desert Storm provides insight into what they may be able to contribute to future missions outside Europe. Two considerations constrain the applicability of this examination to future European force deployments. First, the Europeans deployed forces as part of a multinational coalition and the United States and several other nations provided significant assistance. A European-only deployment will not enjoy this advantage. Second, European force structures have changed since the Gulf War. These changes, discussed in detail in a subsequent chapter, will obviously affect the European forces' capabilities.

This chapter examines the deployment and logistics of the European forces that participated in the Gulf War. It looks at the forces deployed and how quickly they were able to become operational. It examines how the forces reached the Gulf, and their logistics in theater. It also analyzes some of the deployment and logistic constraints that the Europeans faced, and considers the implications of these limitations for future operations.

The chapter also examines the performance of European forces in combat. It first summarizes Operation Desert Storm, providing the context for the European contribution. It then looks at the performance of British forces and intelligence capabilities, and provides an assessment of the British forces' success. A similar analysis of French and other European forces follows. The chapter ends with a discussion of the implications of European forces' performance for future operations.

DEPLOYMENT AND LOGISTICS

Great Britain

Force Deployments. When Kuwait was invaded on 2 August 1990, the British had only limited forces in the area. There were no ground or air assets, although the Royal Navy had several ships in the Persian Gulf. These forces, in the area since the Iran-Iraq reflagging operations, consisted of one destroyer, two frigates, and a supply ship.[1]

By the start of Operation Desert Storm, the British presence was considerably larger. Approximately 45,000 British personnel were deployed, exceeding the number deployed to the Falkland Islands in 1982.[2] In fact, Great Britain sent some 35,000 troops or 23 percent of its ground forces. This was more than half the size of the British Army of the Rhine.

The British commitment to the Gulf was announced on 9 August 1990, and given the name Operation Granby. Initially, Britain reinforced the Royal Navy's assets in the region and sent a squadron of RAF Tornado F-3 fighters and a squadron of Jaguar ground attack aircraft to Saudi Arabia. On 23 August, British forces deployed another squadron of Tornado GR-1s to the region.

Following U.S. Secretary of State James Baker's request for additional allied ground forces on 10 September, the British announced on 14 September that they were going to send the 7th Armored Brigade, stationed in Germany, to the Gulf. Its two armored regiments were equipped with Challenger tanks, and its armored infantry battalion was equipped with Warrior infantry fighting vehicles.

---

[1]Jeffrey McCausland, *The Gulf Conflict: A Military Analysis*, Adelphi Paper 282 (London: Brassey's [UK] Ltd., 1993), p. 9; Andrew Lambert, "The Naval War," in John Pimlott and Stephen Badsey (eds.), *The Gulf War Assessed* (New York: Sterling Publishing Co. Inc., 1992), p. 130.

[2]McCausland, *The Gulf Conflict*, p. 14.

The Brigade's Challenger 1 (Mark 2) tanks were replaced by the more modern Mark 3, and the vehicles were painted in desert camouflage before being shipped out. The first ships carrying the heavy equipment left on 28 September, two weeks after the deployment was announced.

While the equipment was being readied for transport, the brigade units were training in Germany. On 1 October they were put on 72-hour notice to move, and advance parties began to deploy on 10 October. The main party began to deploy on 15 October. Eleven days later, 55 percent of the Brigade's manpower was in theater together with most of its armored vehicles. By the end of October, 80 percent of the Brigade Group had arrived and the three battle groups were complete.

In November 1990, President Bush announced an additional 150,000 American troops were going to be deployed to the Gulf, and the British announced on 22 November that they were going to send HQ 1st (BR) Armored Division to the Gulf. The major units of the division's subordinate 4th Armored Brigade that were going to the Gulf were equipped with Challengers, and the armored infantry battalions were armed with Warriors. In addition, the division was accompanied by a sizable artillery group, a reconnaissance regiment, an air corps regiment, and more logistic units.

During the first week of December, advance parties left for the Gulf. By the end of December, the deployment was more than 50 percent complete, with over 20,000 troops in theater. By 8 January 1991, over 95 percent of 1st (BR) Armored Division was in place. The 4th Armored Brigade, unlike the 7th Armored, was a composite brigade that had not previously trained together. Training for the 4th Armored Brigade began as soon as the troops arrived. By 1 February, the Division was fully operational and complete in its forward concentration areas.

By the start of the ground war, the British had 35,000 troops deployed in the Gulf. In addition to the troops, there were about 170 Challenger tanks and 70 British aircraft in the allied order of battle. The British had also deployed a number of ships to the Gulf. On 31 January, the British had deployed four destroyers, four frigates, five Hunt-class Minehunters, five Royal Fleet Auxiliary (RFA) logistics landing ships, one ocean survey ship (for mine countermeasure [MCM] headquarters and support ships), six replenishment ships, and at least two Oberon-class diesel electric submarines.[3]

Deployment Logistics. The British were able to deploy their air assets quickly into the Gulf. The British first announced that they would deploy a squadron of Tornado air defense aircraft and a squadron of Jaguar ground attack planes to the Gulf on 9 August. Within 48 hours, the squadron of Tornados was operational at Dhahran Air Base, and two aircraft were airborne on an operational mission less than two hours later.[4] By the middle of January, the Royal Air Force had deployed almost 100 aircraft, 14 percent of its total force.[5]

Whereas the British were able to deploy their air assets to the Gulf on almost zero notice, their ground forces took longer to arrive. The 7th Armored Brigade's deployment was announced on 14 September. The first ships carrying heavy equipment docked at Al Jubail on 18 October, more than a month later.[6] It was not until the end of October, more than six weeks after the British troop deployment had been announced, that 80 percent of the 11,500-man deployment had arrived. It took until 16 November before the 7th Armored Brigade was declared operational with sufficient combat supplies and material available to support operations; this was a full two months after the deployment was initially announced. Similarly, it took over six weeks after the announcement of the 4th Armored Brigade's deployment before most of the troops were in theater.

Constraints on Deployment. A number of factors constrained the British deployment to the Gulf. These obstacles not only slowed

---

[3]Bruce W. Watson, "Naval Forces," in *Military Lessons of the Gulf War*, Bruce W. Watson (ed.) (Novato, Calif.: Presidio Press, 1991), pp. 257–259; Lambert, "The Naval War," p. 139.

[4]Rod Alonso, Bruce George, Raimondo Luraghi, Tim Lister, James Piriou, and B. L. Cyr, "The Air War," in *Military Lessons of the Gulf War*, Bruce W. Watson (ed.) (Novato, Calif.: Presidio Press, 1991), p. 62; Ray Sibbald, "The Air War," in *The Gulf War Assessed*, John Pimlott and Stephen Badsey (eds.) (New York: Sterling Publishing Co. Inc., 1992), p. 106.

[5]Alonso et al., "The Air War," p. 62.

[6]Duncan Anderson, "The Build-up," in *The Gulf War Assessed*, John Pimlott and Stephen Badsey (eds.) (New York: Sterling Publishing Co. Inc., 1992), p. 95.

down the deployment, but they affected the force mix that was sent as well. These constraints were both political and physical in nature.

The first factor constraining the British deployment was political: there was a limit to the number of troops that it was politically feasible to send to the Gulf. It was very difficult for General de la Billière to obtain the number of troops that he believed he needed for the operation.

During the Falklands War, Prime Minister Thatcher's motto had been "If we've got it, they can have it."[7] Although she believed that the same principle was being followed in the autumn of 1990, that was not the case. The Ministry of Defense set a ceiling on the number of troops that could be deployed, to limit costs and measure the extent of Great Britain's commitment.[8] Initially, this meant that Whitehall required a detailed justification for every increase above this number. Members of Whitehall then analyzed and challenged these numbers in detail.

There was resistance in Whitehall to sending troops. For example, when the initial decision was made to deploy troops in September, HQ 1(BR) Corps insisted that the 7th Armored Brigade should be at least 12,000 strong. The Ministry of Defense argued for an upper limit of 6000, a force too small to operate independently of American logistic support. Finally, a compromise of 11,500 was reached.[9] In some cases, resistance in Whitehall to sending additional troops was so great that troops were stood up to go to the Gulf and then stood down again. In one instance, troops with their commanding officer flew to Dhahran and had to turn around and reboard the plane to return because their clearance had not come through yet. If a future force deployment does not have significant support within Whitehall, it may mean that the British role in it will remain very small—perhaps only at symbolic levels.

A second British force deployment constraint concerned the amount of equipment that was available to send to the Gulf. HQ 1(BR) Corps

---

[7]As quoted in Peter de la Billière, *Storm Command* (London: HarperCollins, 1992), p. 75.

[8]de la Billière, *Storm Command*, p. 15.

[9]Anderson, "The Build-up," p. 93.

decided that the 7th Armored Brigade would be sent with the best equipment that the British Army of the Rhine possessed. It was also decided that the 7th would ship with enough stores and ammunition to sustain combat for 12 days. As a result, the Royal Electrical and Mechanical Engineers worked around the clock cannibalizing tanks and equipment from other units.[10] General de la Billière commented on the results: the "effort of producing one fully operational armoured brigade had turned the whole system inside-out."[11] In fact, the difficulty in finding enough advanced equipment was so great that "British units deploying from Germany almost required another unit of equal size to ensure that a fully manned and equipped force could be deployed."[12]

The deployments from Germany left the British forces in Germany extremely weakened. Once the 4th Armored Brigade left Germany, the effect on British capabilities in Germany was debilitating: "those units remaining were left with barely enough men to guard their own installations, let alone to carry out any training."[13] As a result, the move "left the British forces in Germany's operational capacity in doubt."[14] Any future British force deployment may face similar constraints.

The third constraint concerned the numbers and skills of the professional personnel available to deploy to the Gulf. The British forces that deployed were professional; no effort was made to augment their strength by activating a significant portion of the Territorial Army. However, these forces lacked some skills, particularly medical ones, to meet anticipated requirements in the Gulf.[15] The government called for volunteers, and eventually even called out Reserve

---

[10]Ibid., p. 93.

[11]de la Billière, *Storm Command,* p. 24.

[12]McCausland, *The Gulf Conflict,* p. 59.

[13]de la Billière, *Storm Command,* p. 24.

[14]McCausland, *The Gulf Conflict,* p. 18.

[15]British planners forecast the anticipated medical team requirements for the deployment of 30,000, and concluded that allowing for 5 percent casualties, a worst-case scenario was 400 casualties per day. This would require no fewer than 49 field surgical teams (FSTs), a requirement that "could not be met from military resources in the United Kingdom." (de la Billière, *Storm Command,* 113.) Remember, though, that the British ended up deploying more than 45,000 personnel to the Gulf.

Forces, but there was still a gap. The British finally asked for (and received) volunteers from other countries.[16]

Medical personnel were not the only specialists that needed augmenting by volunteers. Reservists with other skills and experience, such as military police, public relations, and intelligence, served in the Gulf. The British also did not have enough personnel with language skills available for liaison duties, and they went so far as to "call for volunteers from among English speaking Kuwaiti exiles in Great Britain."[17] A total of 1774 reservists served in Operation Granby; over 90 percent deployed to the Gulf while the others filled gaps that were created by deploying regular troops to the Gulf.

The size of the British army and the number of troops deployed to the Gulf brought up a serious problem: roulement. The British did not have the manpower available to rotate everyone on a four-month cycle: it was "physically impossible."[18] This could have been disastrous, because it meant that it would have been "impossible for us to keep our troops in the desert [two years, which was the length of time that Colin Powell was giving the impression he was willing to stay]."[19] If Saddam Hussein had realized this, he might have devised a strategy requiring the British to keep their troops on indefinitely. Such a plan could have caused serious problems; any future British deployment of similar size may face the same problem.

The final constraint on British deployment concerned the equipment available to transport forces to the Gulf. The British navy and merchant fleet were not large enough to handle British deployments. As a result, the British chartered ships for transport on London's Baltic Exchange. British ships, however, cost more to charter than ships from other countries. The increased costs were such that some

---

[16]These included offers of field hospitals from Sweden, Canada, Norway, and Romania, as well as field surgical teams from Belgium, Denmark, the Netherlands, and Singapore, and a medical team from New Zealand. Ibid., pp. 113–114.

[17]Bruce George, Raimondo Luraghi, Tim Liste, Jane Helwig, Georgia Sakell, Patricia Smith, Bruce W. Watson, and Bruce W. Watson, Jr., "Coalition Diplomacy," in *Military Lessons of the Gulf War*, Bruce W. Watson (ed.) (Novato, Calif.: Presidio Press, 1991), p. 26.

[18]de la Billière, *Storm Command,* p. 93.

[19]Ibid., p. 77.

British owners offered the use of their vessels, only to have them rejected in favor of foreign ships. Of the more than 120 ships from 20 different countries that sailed from England with armor and logistics supplies, only a handful were British.[20]

Logistics in Theater. Initially, the British were dependent on the U.S. Marine Corps for almost everything, particularly food. The British did not have a logistical presence that could adequately support the 7th Armored Brigade when its troops began arriving. However, the logistics units soon arrived and the situation changed by the end of October. British composite rations were much more highly regarded than American MREs (meals ready to eat). In fact, the British traded food for a wide variety of American equipment including machine guns, Humvees, anti-tank missiles, and the American camp-bed, of which some 30,000 found their way into the British lines.[21]

Although the British quickly become self-sufficient, there was still some equipment that they lacked. However, they were able to find ways to supply their troops or borrow needed equipment from the Americans. For example, initially the British did not have any desert pattern uniforms available;[22] they had the uniforms made and early consignments began arriving in the second half of October. Similarly, the British wheeled vehicles that had been designed to bring up supplies of fuel, food, and ammunition in Europe sunk into the sand when carrying loads in the desert. Container trucks designed to drive on tarmac were also ineffective, and as a result the British borrowed a number of M453 tracked vehicles from the United States and quickly shipped them to the Gulf.[23]

Once their logistical system had been geared up, the British were able to supply the needs of their troops. By the start of Britain's Operation Desert Saber on 25 February, 126 ships had delivered over 2500 armored vehicles, 46,000 tons of ammunition, and thousands of tons of other equipment into the theater. The air movement

---

[20]Anderson, "The Build-up," p. 95; de la Billière, *Storm Command*, p. 42; McCausland, *The Gulf Conflict*, p. 14.

[21]Anderson, "The Build-up," p. 96.

[22]Reportedly, the British had sold their stores of desert uniforms to the Iraqis during the Iran-Iraq War.

[23]de la Billière, *Storm Command*, p. 118.

depended on RAF Hercules, VC-10, and Tristar aircraft that made a total of 12,500 sorties. They were supplemented by chartered civilian aircraft that delivered 500 tons of urgent supplies daily. This rate of air movement equaled 10 years of normal peacetime movement by the Royal Air Force.[24]   An official Ministry of Defense account of Operation Granby concluded that "It was, without a doubt, a remarkable achievement."[25]

Equipment. Most of the British equipment had been designed for use in Europe, a very different place from the sands of Saudi Arabia. This had dramatic effects on the life of their equipment. Three examples illustrate the difficulties that the British had using their equipment in the desert. First, as mentioned above, the wheeled supply vehicles that had been designed for use in Europe sank in the sand when fully loaded in the desert. Second, the Challenger tanks' powerpacks (which were the engines and gearboxes combined) failed so often that the British had to curtail training in Saudi Arabia. Finally, the average engine life of a Lynx helicopter in Europe was 1200 hours. In Saudi Arabia, even when fitted with filters, the average life dropped to 100 hours.[26]

The British recognized that they needed to improve their equipment, and started a program to upgrade some of it in theater. They upgraded both their armored vehicles and their airplanes after the deployment had begun. The British decided in December to upgrade the armor of the Challengers and Warriors that had been deployed. They plated on additional armor, and found that these modified vehicles worked better because the armor channeled the sand down, reducing the amount being ingested by the engine. Upgrading these vehicles more than doubled their average powerpack life: in early January, a powerpack gave out every 2.8 kilometers if the entire fleet was moving at once, but by early February that number was up to 6.8 kilometers.

---

[24]McCausland, *The Gulf Conflict*, p. 14.

[25]*Operation Granby: An Account of the Gulf Crisis 1990–91 and the British Army's Contribution to the Liberation of Kuwait* (London: Ministry of Defence, 1991), pp. 3–5.

[26]The average engine life without filters was about ten hours.

The British also were able to upgrade a number of their Tornado aircraft once the air campaign began. During the air campaign, some Tornados flew sorties with Buccaneers. This worked well, because the Buccaneer carried the Pave Spike laser designator that could be used with laser-guided bombs dropped by the Tornados. However, the Pave Spike system could be used only in daylight. The success of laser-guided munitions led to some Tornados being fitted with a Thermal Imaging Airborne Laser Designator (TILAD). The TILAD pods were fully integrated into the Tornado's navigation and bombing system, and were usable at night.[27]

The British also had some ability to immunize their soldiers against biological weapons. They offered voluntary vaccinations against certain bacteriological agents, and more than 10,000 were administered. They also supplied troops in the desert with nerve-agent antidote tablets, designed to reduce the damaging effects of a chemical attack.[28]

France

Force Deployments. When Kuwait was invaded on 2 August 1990, the French had only two corvettes in the area, and no ground or air assets in theater.[29] However, by the start of Operation Desert Saber, France had 13,500 troops and almost 70 planes in theater.[30] More than 6800 naval personnel and 34 ships, about 10 percent of the French navy, participated.[31]

Iraq invaded Kuwait on 2 August, and on 9 August the French sent an aircraft carrier rigged as a helicopter carrier carrying equipment for any ground troops that might be sent to the region. France sent a

---

[27]Alonso et al., "The Air War," pp. 62, 66–67; McCausland, *The Gulf Conflict*, p. 65.

[28]de la Billière, *Storm Command*, pp. 169–170.

[29]McCausland, *The Gulf Conflict*, p. 9; Lambert, "The Naval War," p. 130.

[30]Peter Tsouras, Elmo C. Wright, Jr., and Bruce W. Watson, "Ground Forces," in *Military Lessons of the Gulf War*, Bruce W. Watson (ed.) (Novato, Calif.: Presidio Press, 1991), p. 241.

[31]B. L. Cyr, Bruce W. Watson, Raimondo Luraghi, Bruce George, Tim Lister, and James Piriou, "Naval Operations," in *Military Lessons of the Gulf War*, Bruce W. Watson (ed.) (Novato, Calif.: Presidio Press, 1991), p. 123.

small contingent of 109 men and surface-to-air missiles (SAMs) to Abu Dhabi on 21 August.[32] However, it was not until 14 September, after Iraq seized the French Ambassador's residence in Kuwait and briefly took the French military attaché prisoner, that France committed some 4000 ground troops, along with armor and air support, to the coalition effort. The first French troops, 600 men with 42 Gazelle and Super Puma helicopters, arrived on 23 September. All of the French forces deployed to the Gulf were professional soldiers.[33]

The French commitment of ground troops was called Operation Daguet. It also included sending support troops to Djibouti and the United Arab Emirates (UAE), and establishing an air base in Qatar. On 11 December, France announced that it would reinforce its ground troops. These reinforcements included 155-mm artillery as well as AMX-30B2 tanks and more AMX-10RC wheeled armored vehicles.[34] With the addition of these men and armor, the complexion of the French mission changed.

The reinforcements brought the French deployment up to a division: the Daguet Division. The Daguet Division was designed around the flag and headquarters staff of the French 6th Light Armored Division, with contributions from several other units (most of the units from the *Force d'Action Rapide*).[35] Because the Daguet Division was so "light," a detached brigade of 4500 men from the American 82nd Airborne Division supplemented the Daguet Division.[36]

The French also deployed almost 70 aircraft to the theater. These included Mirage F-1CRs, more than 20 Jaguars, Mirage 2000-2D1s, DC-8 Sarigues, C160s, and C135 FR refueling aircraft. In addition,

---

[32]François Heisbourg, "France and the Gulf Crisis," in *Western Europe and the Gulf*, ed. Nicole Gnesotto and John Roper (eds.) (Paris: The Institute for Security Studies of Western European Union, 1992), p. 23.

[33]Peter Tsouras , Elmo C. Wright, Jr., Bruce George, Tim Lister, James Piriou, and Joe Sanderson, "The Ground War," in *Military Lessons of the Gulf War*, Bruce W. Watson (ed.) (Novato, Calif.: Presidio Press, 1991), p. 81.

[34]James J. Cooke, *100 Miles from Baghdad: With the French in Desert Storm* (Westport, Conn.: Praeger Publishers, 1993), p. 66; David Yost, "France and the Gulf War of 1990–1991: Political-Military Lessons Learned," *The Journal of Strategic Studies* 16, (September 1993), p. 346.

[35]Yost, "France and the Gulf War," p. 346.

[36]Heisbourg, "France and the Gulf Crisis," p. 24.

the French sent eight Mirage F-1Cs to Qatar, and a squadron of 10 Mirage F-1Cs was prepositioned in Djibouti.[37]

In addition to ground and air forces, the French contributed naval forces to enforce the United Nations embargo. France sent seven ships to the Hormuz Strait, and French naval units patrolled key areas of the Straits of Bab el-Mandeb and Tiran.[38] The French also sent naval forces to the Suez Canal. These forces, in addition to British, Spanish, and Italian ships, were able to replace American forces off Libya and demonstrate that NATO still had forces to spare.[39] France also used the aircraft carrier *Clemenceau* to transport trucks, helicopters, and other ground force equipment to Saudi Arabia.[40]

By the start of the ground war, the allied order of battle included 13,500 French troops and 40 tanks.[41] France also supplied more than 56 combat aircraft, a mixture of Mirages and Jaguars.[42] The French had in addition deployed a number of naval ships in support of operations: 13 ships under the Western European Union (WEU) in Operation *Artimon*, including one aircraft carrier, two missile-armed destroyers, four frigates, and a supply ship. Another missile destroyer, two other destroyers, a corvette, an intelligence ship, two supply ships, a repair ship, a tug, and two hospital ships were also deployed.[43]

Constraints on Deployment. Although the French deployments went without any major difficulties, there were a number of factors that constrained the French deployment to the Gulf. These constraints affected the composition of the French forces sent to the Gulf

---

[37]Alonso et al., "The Air War," p. 63. The French government did not deploy its Mirage 2000N aircraft (which had more-advanced penetration capabilities than the Jaguars) because they were all designated for nuclear roles. Yost, "France and the Gulf War," p. 345.

[38]Cyr et al., "Naval Operations," p. 123.

[39]Lambert, "The Naval War," p. 133.

[40]Yost, "France and the Gulf War," p. 344.

[41]International Institute for Strategic Studies, *The Military Balance 1991–1992* (London: Brassey's, 1991), p. 239.

[42]Ibid., p. 240.

[43]Watson, "Naval Forces," p. 259.

and how quickly the forces were deployed. These limitations were both political and physical in nature.

Political factors played a role in the French deployment of forces. The first consideration was Iraq's relationship with France and with members of the Socialist Party. France had been providing military equipment to Iraq—about $25 billion up through 1990.[44] In addition, the French Defense Minister, Jean-Paul Chevènement, had been a founding member of the Iraqi-French Friendship Society.[45] Because Mr. Chevènement was against French military action in the Gulf, President Mitterrand needed Chevènement's presence in the government to help prevent the emergence of a significant anti-war faction in the Socialist Party.[46] Therefore, it was difficult for President Mitterrand to oppose Chevènement and order French ground troops to deploy to the Gulf. However, once Iraqis trespassed onto the French Embassy in Kuwait, Mitterrand was able to commit ground troops.

Because Mr. Chevènement was against Operation Daguet, he was able to hamper the French contribution to the coalition. He deployed French forces so that it was difficult for them to interact with the Western allies. The French forces avoided coalition bases, and deployed their equipment through Yanbu. This explains why the French ground forces were deployed far from other Western allies, and why French aircraft were not stationed at Dhahran with the other allied air forces. It also explains why the French Ministry of Defense announced on 17 January 1991 that French combat aircraft would operate only against targets in Kuwait, and why President Mitterrand later announced that this policy was not accurate.[47] Mr. Chevènement resigned as Minister of Defense on 29 January, and after this "all traces of ambiguity disappeared from France's military posture and activity."[48] Future force deployments might suffer similar complications if Socialist antipathy for collective military action in the region endures.

---

[44]Anderson, "The Build-up," p. 91.

[45]Ibid.

[46]Heisbourg, "France and the Gulf Crisis," p. 24.

[47]Ibid.

[48]Ibid., p. 25.

A second constraint on the French forces concerned the number and skills of the professional personnel available to deploy to the Gulf. When the French announced that they were going to send additional troops to form Division Daguet, they decided to form the Division around the flag of the 6th Light Armored Division. However, more than half of the original 6th Light Armored Division was composed of conscripts who were not required to serve outside of metropolitan France. Although the 1971 conscription law allowed President Mitterrand to send conscripts overseas to fight, the decision was made to send only professional troops to the Gulf.[49] This meant that the draftees had to be replaced with regulars from other units. But few French units had no conscripts, and removing them would deprive most units of their essential support functions.[50] This caused several weeks of organizational confusion and resulted in problems of unit cohesion, training, and readiness.[51] As a result, the French, with an army of 280,000, had more difficulty assembling 13,000 troops than the British had fielding an expeditionary corps of 35,000 from a professional army of 152,900.[52] The use of only professional soldiers brought up another problem: the issue of rotation. France would have experienced "significant problems" if its forces had been required to stay in theater for prolonged periods of time.[53] Any future force deployments may face similar problems.

Logistics in Theater. The French began their deployment by sending the aircraft carrier *Clemenceau* to the area on 9 August. The carrier had problems with its propulsion system, and had to slow to 28 knots.[54] Although it arrived in Djibouti on 22 August, it loitered for several weeks until French ground forces were deployed. Operation Daguet was announced on 15 September, and the *Clemenceau* unloaded its cargo at the Red Sea port of Yanbu on 23 September.

---

[49]Yost, "France and the Gulf War," p. 357.

[50]Ibid., pp. 357–358.

[51]McCausland, *The Gulf Conflict*, p. 59.

[52]Yost, "France and the Gulf War," pp. 357–358.

[53]McCausland, *The Gulf Conflict*, p. 59.

[54]Lawrence Freedman and Efraim Karsh, *The Gulf Conflict 1990–1991: Diplomacy and War in the New World Order* (Princeton, N.J.: Princeton University Press, 1993), p. 116.

The final constraint on the French deployment concerned the equipment available to transport forces to the Gulf. Although the French used some specially chartered French-owned roll-on, roll-off (Ro-Ro) ships to deploy their troops and equipment, the French navy and merchant fleet was not large enough to handle French deployments to the Gulf. As a result, the deployment also involved 282 flights by French military cargo aircraft and two USAF C-5As to complete the mission.[55] In addition, the French had to charter some 49 merchant ships 37 commercial B747s and Airbuses for deployment and sustainment.[56]

It must be noted that the French chose not to utilize allied bases as destinations to ship much of their equipment in theater. This meant that everything had to be moved by truck some 1500 kilometers—a daunting distance in desert conditions—to reach their initial positions on the Western flank of the allied forces.[57] Similarly, the French combat aircraft were stationed in Al-Ahsa rather than in well-equipped Dhahran. In all, between 2 August 1990 and 28 February 1991 France deployed some 16,500 personnel and moved 85,000 tons of freight.[58]

Maintaining their equipment in the desert did not pose major difficulties for the French. French ground forces were familiar with desert deployments, and much of the equipment that was deployed had been designed with the desert in mind. For example, the heat and sand were not a severe problem for the French helicopter force, because French equipment filters were designed for the coarser and more abrasive sand of Chad. Sand ingestion did not cause the loss of a single engine in the *1st Regiment de'Helicoptere de Combat (RHC)* and normal maintenance servicing routines were kept during the operation.[59]

However, some of the equipment that the French deployed to the Gulf was not as modern as the U.S. and UK equipment. For example,

---

[55]Ibid., p.14.

[56]Ibid.

[57]McCausland, *The Gulf Conflict*, p. 14.

[58]Ibid.

[59]Tsouras et al., "The Ground War," p. 100.

some of the French aircraft used the Nadir navigation system, a Doppler-radar system with a greater error potential than the Global Positioning System (GPS) used by other coalition aircraft. The combination of the Nadir navigation system and the absence of radar altimeters meant that French aircraft lacked sufficiently accurate navigation for night operations.[60] Similarly, the French ground forces deployed with older tanks and infantry carriers that were "barely equal to those of the Iraqis."[61]

The French were able to upgrade some of their equipment in theater. French Jaguars benefitted from the addition of American GPS receivers to increase their navigational accuracy.[62] Similarly, the Jaguars were also outfitted with NATO IFF (Identification Friend or Foe) equipment in the interest of their survivability.[63]

Other European Nations

Although the British and French were the primary European contributors to Operations Desert Shield and Desert Storm, other nations also contributed forces. The nature of the contribution varied from country to country, but Italy was the only European nation besides Great Britain and France to send forces that participated in the offensive operations against Iraq. Other countries either contributed to the United Nations blockade of Iraq, NATO reinforcements to Turkey, replacing American naval vessels in NATO deployments so the American ships could deploy to the Gulf, or other noncombat forces.

Italy. The Italian military encountered problems that precluded them from deploying ground forces to the Gulf. The Italian military was undergoing a reorganization from a large conscript army into a smaller professional one. As a result, conscript service obligations were reduced to 10 months—not enough time to train for desert warfare (and the usual conscript training prepared them for emer-

---

[60]Ibid.

[61]James Blackwell, *Thunder in the Desert: The Strategy and Tactics of the Persian Gulf War* (New York: Bantam Books, 1991), p. 172.

[62]Yost, "France and the Gulf War," p. 345.

[63]Ibid.

gencies on the Italian border, not for fighting on the sands of Kuwait).[64]

Italy did, however, mobilize its army to provide protection against anticipated terrorist attacks at home. The Italians drew up a list of 1500 domestic sites to be protected. Since there were so many targets, the Italians mobilized 96 percent of their army, a group totaling 90,000 men, to serve in two groups of 45,000 to protect the potential targets.[65]

Some Italian forces did deploy to the Gulf. Italy sent a squadron of 10 Tornado bombers, reserve teams, repair groups, and a group of engineers to set up a base at Abu Dhabi. The Italian 46th Air Brigade provided two Hercules C-130 aircraft to transport men to and from Italy.[66] The Italian Tornados based in Abu Dhabi were part of the coalition order-of-battle, and took part in Operation Desert Storm.

Italy sent naval forces to the Eastern Mediterranean to guard against Libyan or other hostile action. Italy also deployed a squadron under the WEU consisting of a destroyer, five frigates, three corvettes, two supply ships, and one support ship. Under the command of a rear admiral, this 2400-man contingent included several troops from the San Marco Battalion, the Italian equivalent of Marine Corps.[67]

At Turkey's request, Italy sent troops, several Stinger missile batteries, and six F-104s to Turkey. These forces were part of NATO Allied Command Europe (ACE) Mobile Force (Air), and were not under CENTCOM (Central Command).[68] In addition, two Italian brigades of paratroops and naval infantry (marines) were placed on alert, ready to respond to a NATO defense of Turkey, should it be attacked by Iraq.[69]

---

[64]George et al., "Coalition Diplomacy," p. 24.

[65]Ibid.

[66]Alonso et al., "The Air War," p. 63.

[67]Cyr et al., "Naval Operations," pp. 123–124; Watson, "Naval Forces," p. 259.

[68]Ron Alonso and Bruce W. Watson, "Air Forces," in *Military Lessons of the Gulf War*, Bruce W. Watson (ed.) (Novato, Calif.: Presidio Press, 1991), p. 227; George et al., "Coalition Diplomacy," p. 24.

[69]George et al., "Coalition Diplomacy," p. 24.

Italy also allowed the United States to use Milan's Malpensa International Airport as a major logistical facility for large tanker aircraft that refueled B-52 bombers flying from British bases to Iraqi targets. In addition, Italy authorized the use of Italian military bases and merchant ships to transport American troops and equipment.[70]

Germany.   Germany was slow to support the allied coalition and claimed that its constitution prevented it from deploying military personnel beyond its borders.   However, Germany did deploy 18 Alphajets and 11 Hawk and Roland air defense units to Turkey as part of NATO ACE Mobile Force (Air); these forces were not under CENTCOM.[71]   Germany also provided field medical facilities to forces in the Gulf, and road, rail, air, and sea transports for Allied forces from Germany to the Gulf.[72]

Germany also sent naval forces to the Mediterranean to bolster the defenses there and to allow American naval forces to be redeployed to the Gulf.   In all, Germany sent 19 ships to the Mediterranean to protect the entrance to the Suez Canal, including three minehunters, two minesweepers, a command ship, and an ammunition ship.[73]   These deployments were strictly under NATO auspices and had nothing to do with the coalition.[74]

Other Countries.   In addition to Italy and Germany, Belgium, Denmark, Greece, the Netherlands, Norway, and Spain all contributed forces to the coalition to enforce the UN naval embargo of Iraq.[75]   Belgium, Denmark, the Netherlands, Norway, and Spain sent ships into the Gulf to support the coalition or provided mine-

---

[70]Bruce George and Joe Sanderson, "Financial and Non-Military Support for the Coalition," in *Military Lessons of the Gulf War*, Bruce W. Watson (ed.) (Novato, Calif.: Presidio Press, 1991), p. 221; George et al., "Coalition Diplomacy," p. 24.

[71]Alonso and Watson, "Air Forces," p. 227; McCausland, *The Gulf Conflict*, pp. 20–21.

[72]George and Sanderson, "Financial and Non-Military Support," p. 221.

[73]Watson, "Naval Forces," p. 260.

[74]Bruce W. Watson, Bruce W. Watson, Jr., David Dunphy, Richard DeJong, Brian Gagne, Michael Kirsch, and Yong Pak, "The Effects of the War on Other Nations," in *Military Lessons of the Gulf War*, Bruce W. Watson (ed.) (Novato: Presidio Press, 1991), pp. 193–194.

[75]Department of Defense, *Conduct of the Persian Gulf War: Final Report to Congress* (Washington, D.C.: United States Government Printing Office, 1992), p. 64.

sweepers to clear mines after the hostilities had ended.[76] Bulgaria, Czechoslovakia, Denmark, Hungary, Norway, Poland, Romania, and Sweden all provided medical equipment or noncombat personnel.[77] Belgium, Denmark, Greece, Portugal, and Spain provided transport or logistics support to the coalition.[78] Belgium and the Netherlands deployed forces and equipment to Turkey.[79] Spain also deployed ships to replace the American presence off Libya.[80] Tables 1 and 2 summarize the European contributions.

Table 1

Coalition Air Forces

Country	Fighter/Attack	Tanker	Other	Country	Percent of Total Force
United States	1317	326	178	1821	75.5
Saudi Arabia	276	15	10	301	12.5
Great Britain	78	16	3	97	4.0
France	50	3	1	54	2.2
Kuwait	40	—	—	40	1.7
Canada	26	1	—	27	1.1
Bahrain	24	—	—	24	1.0
Qatar	20	—	—	20	0.8
UAE	20	—	—	20	0.8
Italy	8	—	—	8	0.3
Total	1859	361	192	2412	100.0

SOURCES: International Institute of Strategic Studies, *The Military Balance 1991–1992* (London: Brassey's, 1991), pp. 238–239; Richard P. Hallion, *Storm Over Iraq: Air Power and the Gulf War* (Washington, D.C:. Smithsonian Institution, 1992), p. 158.

---

[76]Lambert, "The Naval War," pp. 134–135; Watson, "Naval Forces," p. 260.

[77]Tsouras, Wright, and Watson, "Ground Forces," pp. 240–241; George and Sanderson, "Financial and Non-Military Support," pp. 221–222; Blackwell, *Thunder in the Desert*, p. 105.

[78]George and Sanderson, "Financial and Non-Military Support," p. 221; Watson, "Naval Forces," p. 260; Alonso and Watson, "Air Forces," p. 227.

[79]McCausland, *The Gulf Conflict*, pp. 20–21; Alonso and Watson, "Air Forces," p. 227; George and Sanderson, "Financial and Non-Military Support," p. 221.

[80]Lambert, "The Naval War," p. 133.

Table 2

Coalition Ground Forces Deployed For Desert Storm and Desert Shield

Country	Troops	Percent of Troops	Tanks	Percent of Tanks
United States	532,000	68.63	2,170	58.10
Saudi Arabia	95,000	12.26	550	14.73
Egypt	40,000	5.16	450	12.05
Great Britain	35,000	4.52	177	4.74
Syria	20,000	2.58	300	8.03
France	13,500	1.74	40	1.07
Pakistan	10,000	1.29	—	—
Kuwait	7,000	0.90	—	—
Qatar	4,000	0.52	24	0.64
UAE	4,000	0.52	—	—
Bahrain	3,500	0.45	—	—
Oman	2,500	0.32	24	0.64
Bangladesh	5,000	0.65	—	—
Morocco	2,000	0.26	—	—
Senegal	500	0.06	—	—
Niger	500	0.06	—	—
Czechoslovakia	350	0.05	—	—
Afghanistan	300	0.04	—	—
Total	775,150	100.00	3,735	100.00

SOURCES: International Institute of Strategic Studies, *The Military Balance 1991–1992*, (London: Brassey's, 1991), pp. 238–239; Peter Tsouras, Elmo C. Wright, Jr., and Bruce W. Watson, "Ground Forces," in *Military Lessons of the Gulf War*, Bruce W. Watson (ed.) (Novato, Calif.: Presidio Press, 1991), pp. 240–241.

Implications

The examination of deployment and logistics above suggests four implications for future European force deployments to the Gulf. First, only a few European countries will probably be willing to deploy combat troops to the Gulf. European countries were willing to send naval forces to reinforce deployments in the Mediterranean so that American ships could deploy to the Gulf, but most were reluctant to commit ground combat forces. However, Europeans were willing to send combat troops (under NATO) to reinforce Turkey should Iraq have tried to invade. European nations also sent ships to enforce the UN blockade of Iraq. European countries were willing to send noncombat troops to the Gulf, either to support troops there or to help with mineclearing operations after hostilities had ended.[81] Only the British, the French, and the Italians took part in the allied offensive. It thus appears that these countries (perhaps with the addition of Germany) are probably the only European nations that will be willing to provide combat forces again should another crisis occur in the Gulf.[82] Of course, collective European military action might not take place at all without effective U.S. leadership.

A second implication concerns the number of combat troops that might be deployed to the Gulf. Overall, European forces made up less than 6 percent of the offensive tank forces, just over 6 percent of the total ground forces, and about 6.5 percent of total air forces. (See Tables 1 and 2.) The French deployment of 13,500 troops was about the smallest size for a deployment to be considered militarily significant.

Great Britain and France faced political problems deploying forces as large as those sent to the Gulf. The second implication for future force deployments is that it will be difficult for either Great Britain or France to deploy significantly larger forces without a great deal of domestic political support. Despite the relatively small size of forces deployed, they represented the upper limit of political consensus on the Gulf crisis.

Just as they produced political stresses, the Franco-British troop deployments also posed operational stresses on their military departments. The force deployments for Operations Daguet and Granby stressed the limits of both countries' professional forces—there were not enough professional forces left to allow rotations. It would have been extremely difficult, and perhaps impossible, for either country to deploy a larger professional force and keep it there for a prolonged period of time. Neither country has the number of professional forces necessary for such a deployment.

---

[81]It is interesting to note that none of the other European navies sent mine countermeasure vessels (MCMVs) to join the British at the head of the Gulf until after hostilities had ended. Lambert, p. 134.

[82]When Iraq moved troops toward the Kuwait border in 1994, Great Britain announced that it would deploy forces to the area. These forces included a frigate, a destroyer, a spearhead battalion (of less than 1000 men from the 45th Commando Royal Marines), and a headquarters planning team.

In the future, the alternative would be to call up reserve forces (an action taken during the Gulf War on a limited scale by Great Britain). However, the leaders of both countries could find it difficult to mobilize sizable reserves without facing domestic opposition. As a result, it is not likely that any future force deployment will be significantly larger unless there is support for calling up military reserves and sending them to the Gulf.

A third implication concerns the use of merchant and commercial shipping to deploy forces. All of the major Western forces (Great Britain, France, and the United States) had to resort to foreign flagged charter vessels to move their equipment. Great Britain and France also had to overcome problems caused by insufficient strategic airlift. Consequently, they had to rely on civilian charter aircraft (and France also got some assistance from the United States).

The reliance on civilian shipping could have caused logistical problems for Great Britain and France. Most ships carrying supplies to the Gulf went singly via the Mediterranean Sea, Suez Canal, and the Red Sea.[83] As a result, if the Iraqis had managed to hijack a consignment of tanks, or if the Yemenis had fired a Silkworm missile at one of the ships as it passed through the Straits of Bab-el-Mandeb, it would have had a significant impact on the build-up. The allies would have had to arrange convoys and divert aircraft from combat air patrols to protect the ships. Although some commercial charters have been arranged to provide shipping during hostilities, a very real and immediate threat to shipping might have caused some firms and their insurance underwriters to breach their contracts or delay releasing ships to the navy. Although the British have contracts in place whereby the Royal Navy operates commercial shipping, the French plans require secure, uncontested ports for its commercial transports. If such facilities should not be available in the theater of operations, the French would unload at an intermediate staging base and use tactical transports to enter the theater—a process that could significantly prolong deployment.

Another factor to consider is the future availability and cost of commercial shipping and air transport. The availability of these trans-

---

[83]McCausland, *The Gulf Conflict*, p. 13.

ports cannot be guaranteed. The cost of these methods of transport, especially if there was a possibility of interdiction, could be significant. For example, the cost of insurance for a civilian aircraft used by the French was 5 million francs after hostilities began.[84] If there is any attempt to attack civilian transports deploying European troops in the future, the costs of deployment could skyrocket and the length of time to deploy could increase significantly.

The final implication is that it would take at least several weeks before the Europeans could deploy a significant force to the Gulf. It took the French nine days before the first of its 4000 troops arrived. It took the British two months after the initial deployment was announced before its brigade was in theater and the deployment was declared operational. Larger force deployments would only have taken more time. In addition, deployment would have taken even longer if supply ships had been interdicted, as discussed above.

Unless future defense programs do the unlikely and provide for more capable force projection, these factors, coupled with the possible problems of not having enough professional forces for a sustained presence, suggest an interesting implication for future deployments: the more troops sent to the region, the longer it takes them to become operational and the shorter is the resulting window for any offensive operation.[85] Any future large European force deployment to the Gulf will have less time to plan, or to undertake, the military mission they have been sent to perform.

PERFORMANCE

Logistics and deployment are not the only factors that may influence the effectiveness of future European force projections into the Gulf region; the performance of troops once they begin offensive operations is another very important factor. We next look at how the Europeans performed during Operation Desert Storm. After describing the operation so that the context can be understood, we will examine how British forces performed in the air, on the ground, and at

---

[84]Ibid., p. 14.

[85]This is, of course, based on the assumption that reserve forces are not mobilized to any significant extent.

sea. We will also look at the performance of French forces and the other European allies. The discussion will end by pointing out some of the implications for future European operations in the region.

An Overview of the Gulf War[86]

The coalition began offensive operations to liberate Kuwait at midnight (GMT) on 16–17 January 1991. These operations included a series of coordinated air strikes by coalition aircraft and Tomahawk cruise missiles against targets in Kuwait and Iraq. The extremely successful initial strikes led some observers to believe that the war could be won in a matter of days without heavy casualties.

The coalition air campaign had four overlapping phases. The first phase was to suppress Iraqi air defenses using American F-111 and F-16 aircraft along with British and Italian Tornados.[87] The second phase was the strategic bombing offensive, which was mainly carried out by F-117 stealth bombers, F-111s, F-15Es, and A-6E Intruder bombers from the U.S. carrier group.

Interdiction was the third phase of the coalition air offensive, paving the way for the ground offensive. The aircraft used in this phase were mainly F-111s, Tornados with Buccaneer laser designator support, Jaguars, A-6s, and A-10s. B-52s bombed troop positions in Kuwait. By 15 February, 27 of the 31 main bridges on the principal Iraqi supply routes had been destroyed, CENTCOM was able to report that the coalition air forces had destroyed 1300 of the 4000 tanks in the Kuwaiti Theater of Operations (KTO), and it was reported in London that almost all of Iraq's oil refining capabilities had been destroyed and the flow of supplies into Kuwait had decreased by 50 percent.[88] The final phase of the air campaign provided support to ground troops.

---

[86]This summary focuses only on those topics relevant to the study.

[87]Some British Tornados were accompanied by Buccaneers for their laser designation systems. Later, when this phase required attacking hardened aircraft shelters, F-117, F-111s, and French Jaguars also participated.

[88]*Operation Granby*, p. 4-2.

The air campaign was not successful in forcing Iraqi troops from Kuwait. The campaign did, however, weaken Iraqi forces in preparation for a quick and impressive ground offensive. The campaign's scope was vast—coalition forces flew an average of more than 2600 sorties per day, equivalent to one plane taking off about every 34 seconds.[89]

Iraq fired 81 Scud missiles during the war. Thirty-eight were fired at Israel, 41 against Saudi Arabia, and two in the direction of Bahrain and Qatar. Because so many of the Scuds were aimed at Israel and accompanied by anti-Israeli rhetoric, the Scuds posed a greater political threat than a military one. Coalition countries sent batteries of Patriot missiles to help counter this threat, and coalition aircraft devoted as many as 300 sorties per day to locate and destroy mobile Scud missile launchers. However, it was the success of the Patriots and the restraint shown by the Israelis that caused the failure of the Iraqi Scud campaign. Since Iraq could not goad Israel into retaliation for the Scud attacks, Iraq lost its chance to alienate Arab participants from their Western coalition partners.

Naval forces were involved in the coalition offensive from the beginning, with the USS *Wisconsin* firing its Tomahawks into Iraq at the start of the offensive. By 22 January, the emphasis of naval operations shifted to the destruction of the Iraqi navy. By 16 February, coalition forces had destroyed at least 60 Iraqi small patrol boats and achieved one of their objectives: the Iraqi navy "had ceased to be effective."[90]

During this period, another goal of the naval forces was to deceive the Iraqi military by convincing them that U.S. marines were going to land in Kuwait. This required British minesweepers to clear lanes for an amphibious landing. It also involved American battleships moving further into the Gulf so they could fire onto Iraqi positions on the coast of Kuwait. Coalition forces were successful in increasing Iraqi concerns about this possible landing.

---

[89]This included reconnaissance flights, combat air patrols and in-flight refueling missions. *Operation Granby*, p. 4-1. Approximately 114,000 offensive air sorties were flown. Yost, "France and the Gulf War," p. 345.

[90]*Operation Granby*, p. 4-3.

The coalition plan for the ground offensive was a double envelopment of Iraqi forces. It was based on a deception plan that was made possible because the air campaign had knocked out Iraqi reconnaissance. Unable to see the entire battle space and deceived by coalition measures meant to give the impression that coalition forces would attack directly across the Kuwaiti border and from the Gulf, the Iraqi command was taken by surprise when the main attack came in the form of a giant "left hook" blow from out of the western desert. The forces that took part in the offensive were the Joint Forces Commands East and North (JFCE and JFCN), both of which were Arab forces; the U.S. Marine Corps of CENTCOM (MARCENT) and the U.S. Army of CENTCOM (ARCENT), consisting of two corps, VII (US) Corps and XVIII (US) Corps (collectively referred to as 3rd (US) Army). British forces took part in operations with the VII (US) Corps while French forces operated with the XVIII (US) Corps.

In the first phase of operations, MARCENT was to launch an attack in the east moving north toward Kuwait City, where the Iraqis were expecting the attack. JFCE would then advance along the coast. Meanwhile, XVIII (US) Corps would set up a screen to protect the coalition's western flank from the Saudi border to the Euphrates. XVIII (US) Corps was to establish a forward operating base inside Iraq so that its helicopters could attack the enemy in northern Kuwait and cut Iraqi lines of communication.

During the second phase of the operation, VII (US) Corps would go into Iraq and then turn east into Kuwait. The JFCN would launch a northward attack into Kuwait at the same time, operating between MARCENT on the right and VII (US) Corps on the left. The final phase would be ARCENT's trapping and destroying the Iraqi Republican Guard Divisions.

The coalition ground offensive began on 24 February. The Marines crossed their line of departure at 0400 hours, and had achieved their objective and taken over 3000 Iraqi prisoners by that evening. The XVIII (US) Corps in the west quickly achieved its first objective, but its advance was slowed when it met resistance at the second objective and could not secure it until the next day. The XVIII (US) Corps established a forward operating base (FOB) within four hours of crossing its Line of Departure, and the Corps' 24th (US) Mechanized Infantry Division began its advance shortly thereafter.

Things were going so well that General Schwarzkopf decided that the VII (US) Corps should begin operations 15 hours early. Throughout the day, the deception continued to be successful, and the Iraqi army began to leave its positions and became vulnerable to coalition aircraft and helicopters.

The second day brought even more coalition successes. The VII (US) Corps had consolidated its bridgehead and begun its first attack on Iraqi positions. The XVIII (US) Corps operation to isolate the KTO was going well. French forces had secured their second objective, the 101st (US) Air Assault Division had cut the main road from Basra to Baghdad, and the 24th (US) Mechanized Infantry Division continued its advance without encountering Iraqi opposition. JFCN had taken its first objective by late afternoon, and JFCE was pushing forward toward Kuwait City. By the end of 25 February, seven Iraqi divisions had been destroyed, more than 25,000 Iraqis had been taken prisoner, and the leading elements of MARCENT were 10 miles from Kuwait City.

By the end of the third day, one Republican Guard Division had been almost destroyed and another division was being attacked by elements of the VII (US) Corps. The 24th (US) Mechanized Division encountered 57 T-72s and destroyed them all. By nightfall the JFCN had secured its final position and JFCE was poised to enter Kuwait City. The US Marines were attacking Kuwait City International Airport and sealing the city. Iraqi soldiers continued to surrender in large numbers, becoming an administrative burden.

The fourth day was the last full day of the coalition ground offensive. Elements of the VII (US) Corps destroyed the Republican Guard Division that they had encountered the day before. The XVIII (US) Corps had completed its encirclement and began an air assault on the Republican Guard. The French maintained their position. The Marines now controlled the entrances to Kuwait City, but were waiting for JFCN and JFCE to liberate the city. Iraqi soldiers were abandoning their equipment and surrendering or posing as civilians. The Iraqis were now in full retreat, and President Bush announced that coalition operations would cease the next day.

During the morning of the fifth day, the VII (US) Corps continued to attack the Republican Guard. The cease-fire took effect at 0800 hours local time—100 hours after coalition forces had launched their ground offensive, and six weeks after the launch of the air campaign.

Great Britain

Air Forces. British RAF Tornados took part in the initial wave of attacks that targeted Iraqi air defenses. These attacks included firing ALARM anti-radar missiles (ARMs) as well as flying night low-level attacks to drop JP233 runway-cratering bombs and 1000-lb bombs on Iraqi airfields.[91] These attacks were designed to harass Iraqi airfield operations rather than close down particular bases. Although the coalition's initial attacks against Iraqi air defenses were incredibly destructive, British commanders decided to change their mission to medium-level attacks and eventually to focus exclusively on interdiction. This decision was made for two reasons.

First, the British JP233 bombs were not causing as much damage as had been expected. Areas that had been hit with the bombs often became operational again within a few hours. Analysis suggested that the sand on which the airfields were built absorbed some of the bombs' blast.[92] The bombs had been designed to break up deep concrete into lumps and slabs that are difficult to repair. Iraqi airfields were apparently built with a thin layer of concrete or tarmac over the sand, which made them easy to flatten out with bulldozers.

Second, the British were experiencing what they considered to be disproportionate losses. The British lost one Tornado in the first 24 hours of the air campaign, and a total of five went down in combat during the first week.[93] None of those five was shot down by anti-aircraft artillery (AAA), and only one of them was listed as going down while carrying out a low-level attack. After the decision was

---

[91]Alonso et al., "The Air War," p. 62; David C. Isby, "Electronic Warfare," in *Military Lessons of the Gulf War*, Bruce W. Watson (ed.) (Novato, Calif.: Presidio Press, 1991), p. 162.

[92]de la Billière, *Storm Command,* p. 209.

[93]Alonso et al., "The Air War," p. 65; Sibbald, "The Air War," p. 114.

made to stop flying low-level attacks, only one more Tornado was lost during the rest of the campaign.[94]

After 23 January, British planes spent the next two- to three-week period flying medium-level attacks mainly using ballistic freefall 1000-lb bombs on a variety of large-area targets. British Tornado crews had very little training for this type of attack. General de la Billière characterized these operations as "largely ineffective."[95]

During this period, the British sent Buccaneers to the Gulf to act as laser-designators for the Tornados.[96] The Buccaneers were fitted with Pave Spike laser-designator pods and could act as a target (laser) designator for Tornados and Jaguars. In addition, each Pave Spike Buccaneer could carry four laser-guided bombs (LGBs) or Anglo-French television-guided anti-radiation Martel missiles and was capable of conducting strikes alone.[97] The combination of Tornados and Buccaneers quickly proved successful.[98] By the end of the fourth week of the war, some 60 percent of Tornado sorties were using LGBs, and more Buccaneers were deployed.[99]

The success of the laser-guided munitions meant that the Tornados could be effective for ground interdiction. The British mission for the last three weeks thus concentrated on bombing more point targets, such as bridges and airfield facilities. During this period some

---

[94]Of the six British Tornados that were lost in combat, two flew into the ground, one was destroyed by a mis-released bomb, and three were hit by surface-to-air missiles. de la Billière, *Storm Command,* p. 204.

[95]Ibid., p. 228. The author did, however, point out that American aircraft "when not using precision-guided (so-called 'smart') bombs, were having no better success."

[96]When the British initially suggested deploying Buccaneers in November, they had been assured that there were enough American designators for the British aircraft. However, the American planes had been diverted to help with the search for Scud launchers. As a result, the British Buccaneers were not initially available in theater. Ibid., pp. 229–230.

[97]Alonso et al., "The Air War," p. 76.

[98]In fact, on their first live sortie together four Tornados and three Buccaneers were able to destroy an important bridge over the Euphrates. de la Billière, *Storm Command,* p. 230.

[99]Alonso et al., "The Air War," p. 67.

Tornados were upgraded with their own thermal-imaging airborne laser designators, giving them a night capability.[100]

The British also used Jaguars based in Muharraq for interdiction and close air support. The Jaguars attacked a variety of targets in the KTO, including supply dumps, surface-to-air missile sites, artillery, and Silkworm missile sites. They also successfully attacked Iraqi naval patrol boats and landing craft. They flew both day and night missions, and attacked from a high altitude with tactics very different from the ones they had practiced during NATO training.[101]

In all, the British RAF flew some 6000 sorties between 17 January and 28 February, including 2000 offensive sorties by Tornado GR1 and Jaguar aircraft. The British lost seven Tornados in combat, six of them during the first week of the campaign.[102] The British used their air assets for air defense, offensive counter air and air interdiction, tactical reconnaissance, and Nimrod maritime reconnaissance operations. Tornado F3s flew more than 2500 operational combat air patrol sorties, of which over 700 were flown during the war. Although the British RAF had only 3.25 percent of the air assets in theater, they flew 4.8 percent of all operational sorties.[103]

Naval Forces. British naval forces participated in offensive operations in the Gulf and helped the coalition in two other ways. First, they sent ships to enforce the UN embargo of Iraq. The embargo was very effective, severely restricting Iraqi seaborne trade.[104] Second, they sent forces to replace American ships in the Mediterranean. These reinforcements allowed American ships to deploy to the Gulf.

British naval forces performed well in the Gulf. One of the most notable naval actions took place on 29 January. A convoy of 17 Iraqi patrol boats and assault crafts was detected by a British frigate's

---

[100]Sibbald, "The Air War," p. 117.

[101]de la Billière, *Storm Command,* p. 230.

[102]Alonso and Watson, "Air Forces," pp. 228–229.

[103]de la Billière, *Storm Command,* p. 270.

[104]Department of Defense, *Conduct of the Persian Gulf War,* pp. 76–77. With Iraq denied the use of Syrian ports, the British patrol off of the Iraqi port of Al Faw effectively choked off Baghdad's access to sea-transported goods. Only a little smuggled material trickled into Iraq through the Jordanian port of Al Aqabah.

radar.[105] Lynx helicopters equipped with Sea Skua missiles were scrambled and sank four of the boats and damaged another 12.[106] Later in the day, Lynx helicopters sank another large patrol boat.

The next day, coalition naval forces detected a more substantial convoy, including three ex-Kuwaiti TNC 45s, three Polnocny landing craft, and a Type 43 minelayer. Sea Skua missiles knocked out all seven ships, and RAF Jaguars destroyed the Polnocnys.[107] Later in the day, Lynx helicopters took out two more minelayers and an ex-Kuwaiti TNC 45.[108] During the engagements of 29 and 30 January, British Lynx crews scored hits with 18 of 25 fired Sea Skua missiles and maintained flying rates about three times normal.[109] All of the Iraqi missile-capable aircraft had been destroyed by 3 February, and coalition control of the Gulf was declared on 8 February. British forces had destroyed about 25 percent of the Iraqi navy.[110]

During this period, minesweepers were clearing mine lanes in preparation for an amphibious assault. British minesweepers played a significant role in these operations. The Americans were using helicopters, surface ships, and divers to clear mines, but the British had more experience, and their Hunt-class MCMVs were much more effective.

On 14 February, the allied fleet began to move north behind British Royal Navy minesweepers. On 18 February, two American warships struck mines when they strayed from the cleared path.[111] By 23 February, a fire support area was cleared, and the first battleship was able to take position to begin bombardment of Iraqi positions. By the cease-fire on 28 February, the MCMVs had located and disposed

---

[105]The convoy was apparently involved in the Iraqi attack against Khafji. Ground forces attacked the city in order to cut off a Marine Corps' unit by land, and these forces were apparently going to land in the rear of the town, encircling the marines.

[106]*Operation Granby*, p. 4–3. Coalition aircraft destroyed the entire convoy: 14 boats were sunk and three were driven ashore. Lambert, "The Naval War," p. 137.

[107]The TNC 45s were sunk by A-6s. Lambert, "The Naval War," p. 138.

[108]*Operation Granby*, p. 4–3.

[109]de la Billière, *Storm Command*, p. 251.

[110]Ibid.; *Operation Granby*, p. 4–3.

[111]Cyr et al., "Naval Operations," p. 126.

of 191 mines.[112] The five British MCMVs enjoyed such a great success that when coalition forces returned to Kuwait, Rear Admiral Taylor, USN, signaled a British MCMV to take the lead because "the fleet was used to following a 'Hunt.'"[113]

British Type 42 guided-missile destroyers also proved effective during the war. The British destroyers were integrated into the U.S. Navy's anti–air warfare defensive organization. They controlled carrier fighter combat air patrols for local defense and ensured that Iraqi aircraft were not attempting to use returning allied formations to cover a surprise attack.[114] On 25 February, a British destroyer providing air support to a U.S. battleship detected a Silkworm missile launched from the coast and fired two Sea Dart surface-to-air missiles. One of these missiles destroyed the only Silkworm to threaten allied forces.[115]

The British forces relied on the Inmarsat satellite for communication and experienced some problems communicating between their military headquarters in Riyadh and British ships in the Gulf.[116] The system was designed to be used by merchant vessels and provided poor connections between Riyadh and ships in the Gulf. Although General de la Billière used Inmarsat to inform British Commodore Craig when the attack would begin,[117] as a result of this communication limitation, he later delegated a great deal of authority concerning naval operations to Commodore Craig.

Ground Forces. The 1st (BR) Armored Division made up the British contribution to Desert Saber. Although the division—subordinated to the VII (US) Corps—was under American tactical control, the British retained the right of veto, which would enable them to rescind the transfer of power and take back control if they so

---

[112]Ibid. The Iraqis had laid over 1200 mines off of the Kuwaiti coast. By 26 March, over 270 of them had been destroyed. Cyr et al., p. 127; Lambert, "The Naval War," p. 141.

[113]As quoted in Lambert, "The Naval War," p. 141.

[114]Cyr et al., "Naval Operations," p. 128.

[115]The other missile fell harmlessly into the sea.

[116]de la Billière, *Storm Command,* pp. 59, 151, 197.

[117]The message was scrambled using the British system Brahms.

desired.[118] The British requested additional fire support and were given a United States National Guard artillery brigade composed of a Multiple Launch Rocket System (MLRS) battalion and additional guns.[119]

Once the British forces entered Iraq, their goal was to defeat the enemy's tactical reserves on the eastern flank in order to protect VII (US) Corps' right flank. The British plan was to press forward as quickly as possible. British forces were to destroy enemy tanks and artillery as they found them, but to bypass enemy infantry positions. Their objectives—concentrations of enemy forces—were named after metals: Bronze, Copper, Steel, and Zinc.

The 7th (BR) Armored Brigade rolled forward quickly toward its first objective, Copper North, stopping briefly only when GPS satellites were below the horizon. Elements reached Copper North at 2100 hours and discovered a sizable enemy position. They called fire from British 155-mm guns and the American MLRS system, and the enemy tanks retreated.

The 7th (BR) Armored continued to push forward, and at about 0300 hours it decided to stop its advance. As the men were sitting in the dark, they began to see through their thermal and optical gunsight (TOGS) system that Iraqi tanks were setting up a counterattack. Since the forces of the 7th had the advantage of being able to see the enemy without being seen, they waited until the Iraqi tanks were within about 2500 meters and opened fire. They destroyed 10 Iraqi tanks without taking a single hit from the Iraqi main armaments; the other tanks turned and retreated.[120]

The 7th advanced to its next objective, Zinc, a main Iraqi stronghold with large numbers of tanks and infantry in berms. During a sandstorm at first light, elements of the 7th closed within 400 meters of the Iraqis and opened fire. By 0530 hours on G+2 the 7th had cleared Zinc and captured 30 tanks, destroyed 16 armored personnel carriers

---

[118]de la Billière, *Storm Command,* pp. 79–80.

[119]Ibid., pp. 148, 284.

[120]Ibid., p. 283.

(APCs) and taking 1850 enemy prisoners of war.[121] The 7th then pushed on to Platinum. The enemy began surrendering en masse, and the British quickly overran the position. The 7th encountered some resistance at objective Lead, but Lead was secured about three hours after Platinum.

The 4th (BR) Armored Brigade encountered unexpected enemy positions as it moved toward its first objective, Bronze. Forces engaged the units and destroyed a signals and artillery unit and an artillery battery. The 4th secured Bronze by 0230 hours on G+2 after destroying 12 enemy tanks, 11 guns, and some additional 20 vehicles.[122] They then cleared the area for occupation by some of the 1st (BR) Armored Division's logistical units.

The brigade then moved on to its next objective, Copper South, which was believed to contain an artillery battery. In reality, the objective contained a heavy battle group of about 25 tanks and APCs, guns, and logistics vehicles. The 4th encountered the enemy at about midnight on G+2 and put the advantage afforded them by their TOGS to good use. By 0530 hours they had secured Copper South. They captured or destroyed 50 armored vehicles and took a number of POWs, including two Iraqi divisional commanders.[123]

The 4th then moved on to objective Brass, which contained most of an Iraqi armored brigade. Challengers moved around the Iraqi positions, and were able to identify and destroy six T-55s quickly. The Iraqis were not expecting an attack from this direction, and were facing the wrong way. Warriors were called forward and infantry cleared the enemy trenches. By 1200 hours, the 4th had taken Brass and had destroyed more than 30 tanks and almost 50 armored personnel carriers.[124] By 1530 hours, it had secured its next objective, Steel, losing nine men to friendly fire.[125]

---

[121] *Operation Granby*, p. 5–17.

[122] Ibid.

[123] Ibid.

[124] de la Billière, *Storm Command*, p. 288.

[125] The men were mistakenly attacked by an American A-10. See Ibid., pp. 288–292.

The Iraqis had begun retreating northward by this time, the afternoon of G+2. The British forces prepared to switch to pursuit, but first the 4th (BR) Armored Brigade had to secure objective Tungsten, which required crossing over an above-ground pipeline. The division's heavy artillery, plus MLRS and M110 203-mm self-propelled howitzers from the U.S. National Guard 142nd Artillery Brigade, provided fire support. The bombardment lasted through the night, with infantry pushing forward to clear enemy positions. By dawn, only one enemy position remained, and three engagements coupled with loudspeaker psyops broadcasts convinced the enemy to surrender.

By this time the British had reached a position in less than two days that the British division and brigade commanders had estimated would take from four to ten days.[126] The 1st (BR) Division had to pause to remain clear of the lines of advance for the 1st (US) and 3rd(US) Armored Divisions. The British were later given the order to advance to objective Varsity inside Kuwait. They secured Varsity by 1230 hours on G+3. They encountered little resistance—the objective had already been abandoned by the Iraqis.

The 1st (BR) Division received new orders at 2230 hours on G+3—to attack east and cut off routes from Kuwait City that the Iraqis could use to retreat north. Shortly after midnight, the news came of a possible cease-fire beginning at 0800 hours. The 1st British began its advance to the Basra-Kuwait road and reached the objective at 0725 hours.

During the 100 hours of Operation Desert Saber, the British division had destroyed almost three armored Iraqi divisions, taken over 7000 Iraqi prisoners, and captured more than 4000 pieces of equipment and 2000 small arms.[127] Forty-seven British soldiers were killed, and 43 were wounded.[128]

Three pieces of allied equipment made a significant contribution to the success of Desert Saber. The first was allied artillery, especially the American MLRS and the British 155-mm guns. These artillery systems were devastating to the Iraqis. For example, British interro-

---

[126]Ibid., p. 293.

[127]*Operation Granby*, p. 5-20.

[128]Tsouras, Wright, and Watson, "Ground Forces," p. 247.

gation teams learned that before the British assault on objective Tungsten, the enemy had 76 guns. By the end of the bombardment, only 17 of the guns remained and 90 percent of the crews were dead or wounded.[129]

The second piece of allied equipment that made a significant contribution was the Global Positioning System. British tank commanders used GPS to locate their positions to an accuracy within about 15 meters.[130] These systems proved invaluable in the desert, where the terrain did not provide significant landmarks. In addition, GPS allowed the British to operate at night and through rain and sand storms. The system's only drawback was that its satellites were occasionally below the horizon.

The third system that proved extremely useful was the thermal and optical gunsight used by British Challengers. These systems allowed tank crews to operate in the dark and gave tank commanders the ability to pick up enemy vehicles at a distance of 2500 to 3000 meters.[131] Challengers were able to use TOGS to fire accurately at Iraqis well before the Iraqi gunners could even see them. The combination of GPS and TOGS meant that the British could approach Iraqi forces and fire on them before the Iraqis realized the British were even in the area.

Special Forces. British special forces operated behind enemy lines during the Gulf War. The plan originally called for British special forces to distract the Iraqis from the Gulf and make them believe that some major operation was being prepared on the right flank.[132] Their primary objectives were to attack communications and roads, with a secondary objective of deception and general harassment of Iraqi forces.[133] Later, locating mobile Scud missile launchers became a priority.

---

[129]de la Billière, *Storm Command,* p. 293.

[130]Ibid., p. 282.

[131]de la Billière, *Storm Command,* p. 282; *Operation Granby,* pp. 5–18.

[132]de la Billière, *Storm Command,* p. 188.

[133]Ibid., p. 195.

British special forces achieved many of their objectives. The British Special Air Service (SAS) mined bridges, destroyed microwave towers and communication facilities, cleared mines in the Gulf, contaminated Iraqi fuel, and picked up more than 30 documents that gave intelligence about enemy dispositions and logistics plans.[134] Members of the British Special Boat Service (SBS) also participated, blowing up substantial parts of the communications network between Baghdad and Iraqi troop deployments.[135] In addition, the SAS played a role in the air campaign, using laser-designators to illuminate buildings and facilities, as well as locating and destroying mobile Scud missile launchers.[136] Four British SAS members died during the war.[137]

Intelligence. Once the war started, the British had some tactical reconnaissance capability. Some British Tornados made low-level sweeps with infrared and video recording sensors, flying at night. Initially they flew in pairs, but they had to change tactics to become more unpredictable. They flew over enemy territory to gather intelligence against Scud mobile launchers, Iraqi positions, supply routes, and bridges for bomb damage assessment.[138] In addition, some British Nimrods performed electronic reconnaissance.[139]

The British were dependent on the United States for strategic intelligence. The United States was able to use satellites, the airborne warning and control system (AWACS) and other technical means to gather accurate and timely intelligence that the British could not get elsewhere.

Assessment. British air forces were able to perform both air defense suppression and interdiction missions. During the campaign the Royal Air Force fired more than 100 ALARM ARMs.[140] British

---

[134]Ibid., p. 221; Tsouras et al., "The Ground War," p. 95.

[135]de la Billière, *Storm Command,* pp. 218–219.

[136]Alonso et al., "The Air War," p. 121.

[137]de la Billière, *Storm Command,* p. 262.

[138]Alonso et al., "The Air War," p. 67.

[139]Lambert, "The Naval War," p. 135; Isby, "Electronic Warfare," p. 158.

[140]Isby, "Electronic Warfare," p. 162.

Tornados, when outfitted to deliver laser-guided bombs, were very effective in destroying their targets.

British naval forces also performed well in offensive operations. The British Sea Skua missile was particularly effective in destroying Iraqi ships. British MCMVs were also very capable, as were British missile destroyers. Additionally, British naval forces integrated well with American forces operating in the Gulf.

British ground forces also performed well in the Gulf. The British commanders had been given clear objectives and had the forces to achieve them. British forces were able to advance quickly, and they overcame almost three Iraqi divisions. The Challenger tanks proved effective despite reservations about their reliability that some had before offensive operations began. The American artillery brigade, especially the MLRS, provided an important complement to British fire support. British special forces accomplished a number of difficult missions, from locating mobile Scud launchers to blowing up a communications network linking Iraq to Kuwait. They were also able to gather intelligence on Iraqi dispositions.

France

Air Forces. French aircraft also participated in the coalition air campaign. As early as daylight on 17 January, French Jaguars bombed the Al Jabar airbase and Scud missile silos. Mirage 2000s flew defensive missions over Saudi Arabia and strikes on munitions depots, naval bases, and other targets. The French intensified their attacks on 23 January, and began flying two daily missions carrying different armaments against targets. By 12 February, the French air force had delivered 1000 250-kilogram bombs, and by 18 February the Mirage 2000s had been in the air more than 1000 hours.[141] The French lost only one aircraft, a Jaguar on the first day of the air campaign.[142] From 17 January to 23 February, French aircraft performed 1387 offensive air sorties,[143] or about 1.2 percent of the total 114,000

---

[141]Alonso et al., "The Air War," p. 65.

[142]Alonso and Watson, "Air Forces," p. 228.

[143]Yost, "France and the Gulf War," p. 345.

offensive air sorties flown by the allies during the six weeks of the war.

Naval Forces. France's aircraft carriers did not participate in offensive combat operations, although French ships apparently did support the coalition offensive.[144] France sent seven ships to the Hormuz Strait, and French naval units patrolled key areas of the Hormuz Strait and the Straits of Bab el-Mandeb and Tiran. The French also sent naval forces to the Suez Canal. These forces, in addition to British, Spanish, and Italian ships, were able to replace American forces off Libya. French ships also helped enforce the embargo of Iraq. They conducted more than 7500 missions (patrols, interceptions, and boardings) enforcing the embargo.[145]

Ground Forces. The French contribution, Division Daguet, was subordinated to the XVIII (US) Corps. Although the division was under American tactical control, the French were able to take back control if they believed it was necessary. The coalition plan called for the French division to help achieve the objective of isolating the KTO by securing the coalition's left flank. Their mission was to take and clear an escarpment, and then to move north to take and secure the road junction and airfield at As Salman. Their main opposition was the 45th (Iraqi) Infantry Division, which was positioned between the escarpment and As Salman. Intelligence suggested that the division was short one infantry brigade.[146]

The French crossed their line of departure at 0530 hours on the first day of the land war. They headed north toward the escarpment and took it almost uncontested.[147] They found large numbers of uniforms, weapons, and even water; the Iraqi soldiers had apparently

---

[144]President Mitterrand has stated that several French ships participated in naval air operations in the north of the Gulf. Yost, p. 343. Presumably the ships' participation was limited to secondary and support roles; they are not listed.

[145]Cyr et al., "Naval Operations," p. 125.

[146]Most intelligence estimates showed that the 45th had two infantry brigades (instead of the customary three), one artillery brigade, and an indeterminate number of tanks in the area. Cooke, *100 Miles from Baghdad*, p. 60.

[147]Ibid., p. 100.

just deserted.[148]   The French continued toward the Iraqi division between them and As Salman.

The 45th (Iraqi) Infantry Division, designated objective Rochambeau, was at 75 percent strength after the air campaign. The Iraqis had apparently convinced themselves that any allied attack would come down the hardtop road leading toward their position. They had ignored the possibility that an attack could come from the desert, and the 45th did not conduct adequate reconnaissance. The French forces did not approach on the road, and took the Iraqis by surprise.

The 45th (Iraqi) Division's defense of its positions was not spirited. French helicopters approaching Rochambeau encountered large groups of Iraqis waving white flags even before tanks and infantry had closed with the main enemy force. After an artillery bombardment, the allies attacked from an angle and the rear, taking the main Iraqi forces by surprise. Many of the 45th Division's revetted tanks and personnel carriers could only traverse their guns a few tens of degrees, and therefore could not put up an effective defense. Although the Iraqis initially put up some resistance, they surrendered by the hundreds and then the thousands. In fact, so many Iraqis surrendered that the Division Daguet had to halt its advance; they stopped counting that afternoon when the total of prisoners had soared above 1900.[149] The commander of the U.S. airborne brigade commented that "every soldier I saw surrendered."[150]

The French forces continued to the town of As Salman, encountering only scattered Iraqi resistance and taking prisoners. When they entered the town, it was deserted of soldiers except for a few who had been separated from their company and found themselves ringed by allied troops and forced into the town.[151] In fact, the most significant threat confronting them in As Salman were unexploded cluster bombs (CBUs). Seven American engineers and two French members of the *Commandos de Récherche et d'Action dans la Profondeur* were

---

[148]The weapons they found included such things as AK47 assault rifles and RPG 7 antitank rocket launchers, as well as large quantities of ammunition for both. Some of the weapons and uniforms were brand new and had never been fired or worn. Ibid.

[149]Ibid., p. 110.

[150]As quoted in Blackwell, *Thunder in the Desert*, p. 196.

[151]Cooke, *100 Miles from Baghdad*, p. 130.

killed in incidents probably caused by unexploded CBUs.[152] The Division Daguet's headquarters moved into As Salman. Some French forces advanced farther north and stopped, securing their positions until the cease-fire.

The French forces neutralized an Iraqi infantry division, suffering only minimal casualties: two dead and 25 wounded.[153] Three factors contributed to the Division Daguet's success. The first factor was detailed operational and tactical planning. The French were able to fight a series of battles requiring intricate maneuvers and co-ordination of helicopters, artillery, tanks, and infantry—capabilities well within French competence. Intelligence allowed Daguet's forces to approach Iraqi defensive lines at an angle. If the Division Daguet had come at them straight on, the Iraqi tanks could have caused considerable damage, especially to infantry in light armored vehicles.[154]

Second, the coalition won the reconnaissance-counterreconnaissance battle. The Iraqis were almost blind to the movements of the Division Daguet. They were forced to react, rather than taking the initiative to attack. In addition, the 45th (Iraqi) Infantry Division had ignored the expanse of desert surrounding it and concentrated on defending the lone road leading to their position. If the Iraqis had been reconnoitering the desert for the attack that they knew had to be coming, they could have had enough warning to change their defensive orientation to meet the Division Daguet head-on. Fortunately this did not happen, and Division Daguet retained the element of surprise.

A final factor was the morale of the Iraqi army. If the Iraqis had fought instead of surrendered, the battle could have been much more costly for the French. For example, one observer noted that if the Iraqis had not retreated from the escarpment, a "spirited defense could well have halted the French advance."[155]

---

[152]Ibid., p. 131. The cause of the explosion that killed the French forces was never made clear.

[153]Tsouras, Wright, and Watson, "Ground Forces," p. 247.

[154]Cooke, *100 Miles from Baghdad*, p. 140.

[155]Ibid., p. 101.

Intelligence. The French were dependent upon the United States for photographic intelligence of the area of operations before the war began and for Intelligence Preparation of the Battlefield (IPB). IPB requires trained personnel to interpret a series of overlays depicting all manner of information about the battlefield and the enemy: terrain, enemy positions, and enemy patterns of movement. Unfortunately, the French had only a limited number of support personnel to meet their needs. These personnel were "taxed to the limit," and even the addition of three American personnel "could not solve the problem of information flow."[156]

The French forces deployed to the Gulf with some communications intelligence (COMINT) capabilities, including a DC-8 Sarigue, an EC-160 Gabriel, and two modified SA330 Puma helicopters, as well as an electronic research ship to gather intelligence on the Iraqis.[157] Mirages also conducted reconnaissance against Iraq.[158] However, once the war began, the French were dependent upon the Americans for accurate and timely strategic data.

Assessment. French forces performed well in the Gulf War. French naval forces enforced the UN embargo of Iraq. French ships replaced American forces elsewhere, allowing those forces to deploy to the Gulf. French aircraft flew almost 1400 offensive sorties and only lost one aircraft. However, French aircraft were not capable of navigating at night and French forces were assigned only day missions. If coalition forces had not had enough sufficient aircraft, this could have caused problems.

The French deployed a light, mobile ground force to the Gulf, Division Daguet. The French forces were assigned to screen the coalition's west flank, and performed the mission quickly, neutralizing an Iraqi infantry division. However, the Division's success rested upon good planning and intelligence—intelligence that the French were dependent on the United States to provide. In addition, if the

---

[156]Ibid., pp. 57–58. However, the situation became easier after the XVIII sent electronic warfare teams to the Division Daguet headquarters. These teams had little to do, and were able to contribute to the IPB effort. Ibid., pp. 82–83.

[157]The research ship was reportedly configured for electronic support measures. Isby, "Electronic Warfare," pp. 158, 159.

[158]Alonso et al., "The Air War," p. 63.

Iraqi forces had put up significant resistance, the French would have suffered considerably more casualties.

Other European Nations

Italian aircraft participated in the allied air campaign.   Italian Tornados began flying offensive missions on 17 January, and lost only one Tornado.   In addition to the bombing missions against Iraqi targets, the Italian air force also flew defensive air missions to protect Italian ships.   The offensive missions consumed 2100 flying hours, and the defensive ones an additional 2000 hours.[159]   In total, Italian planes flew 226 missions against Iraqi targets in the vicinity of Basra, the Iraqi-Kuwaiti border, and inside Kuwait.[160]

Italy also sent naval forces to the Gulf under the command of a rear admiral.   The squadron consisted of a destroyer, five frigates, three corvettes, two supply ships, and one support ship.[161]   The Italian naval forces provided protection to American carriers and were ready to support amphibious operations.   Italian helicopters flew 50 missions protecting ships and identifying mines and suspect ships.[162] The Italian contingent was reduced on 15 April to three minesweepers, two frigates, and a support ship.   Denmark, the Netherlands, and Norway also sent small naval contingents to the Gulf.[163]

Assessment.   It is difficult to assess the performance of these European forces because they performed mainly noncombat roles. However, it became clear that coordination was a problem in naval operations.   Among the coalition naval forces, the American, Australian, British, and NATO forces adopted standard NATO operating procedures and secure signaling systems, whereas other countries had to rely on ship-to-ship radio.[164]   This restricted the oper-

---

[159]Ibid., p. 65.

[160]Ibid.

[161]Cyr et al., "Naval Operations," p. 123.

[162]Ibid., p. 128.

[163]Watson, "Naval Forces," p. 260.

[164]Lambert, "The Naval War," p. 132.

ating capabilities of some naval forces. In fact, it was such a large constraint that one British naval authority commented that the European naval collaboration was not effective and only the British, Dutch, and possibly the Australians were able to work within the U.S. Tactical Naval Command.[165]

Implications

Examination of the European contingent's performance suggests two implications for future out-of-area operations. The first is that coordination between countries is difficult. Although naval coordination between British and American forces worked well, other European forces were constrained by the lack of secure communication systems. In addition, they did not share the same standard operating procedures or even rules of engagement. There may be a difficulty in forming an armada based upon the naval forces of several European countries.

The identification of forces also presented difficulties of coordination. Because there was such a mix of different forces from so many countries, it was often difficult to distinguish between friend and foe. There were incidents of troops being killed by forces from other friendly nations as a result. In addition, the French deployed Mirage F-1s, the same type of aircraft that had been purchased by Iraq. This, plus that the fact that not all coalition aircraft initially had NATO IFF equipment, made it more difficult to distinguish between friendly and hostile aircraft. If the coalition air campaign had not been so successful in destroying the Iraqi air forces, this could have posed a much more significant problem.

The second implication is that any similar European power projection operations in the future may depend upon non-European capabilities for their success. This stems from the fact that the European forces could not have succeeded without help. The European ground forces were assigned missions that they could achieve. The French were assigned a screening operation, which required the addition of an American airborne infantry brigade to Division Daguet. Similarly, an American artillery brigade supple-

---

[165]McCausland, *The Gulf Conflict*, p. 17.

mented the British division during the ground offensive. Without these additional non-European forces and the low morale of Iraqi forces, the European forces would not have achieved the successes they experienced during Operation Desert Saber.

The air campaign could not have succeeded with only French, British, and Italian planes. The French Jaguars were limited to flying during the day, and French Mirage F-1s were not flown on offensive missions because Iraq possessed the same aircraft. The British Tornados, Jaguars, and Buccaneers performed well once they could use laser-guided bombs, but their numbers were limited. The European forces arrayed were not capable of completing all four phases of the air campaign successfully. Left to their own devices, the Europeans either would have had to bring a different mix of aircraft in larger numbers, or they would have had to organize the air campaign differently.

The British and the French were also dependent on the United States for intelligence. Although the European forces had some means of gathering intelligence, this ability was limited. The success of their missions depended on successful intelligence preparation of the battlefield before the offensive began and timely and accurate intelligence while it was under way. The Europeans did not have the capabilities to provide this intelligence, and they relied on the United States for it. If the United States had not been able to provide the necessary intelligence, the Europeans would not have been able to provide it for themselves.

Chapter Three

FUTURE MILITARY DIMENSIONS OF SOUTHWEST ASIA

What circumstances will confront the Europeans or any outside forces if they try to intervene in Southwest Asia over the near term? At least three factors bear directly on the answer to this question. First, the sources of conflict in the region; second, the strategies that adversaries might adopt to oppose the Western presence; and third, the armament and modernization programs of the regional predatory, non-status-quo states. The approach taken here is to survey each factor with an eye toward developing demanding, yet plausible, conditions. Readers needing official estimates of information for specific forecast years should consult appropriate intelligence documents.

Sources of conflict abound in the region. This study makes no attempt to foresee the specific circumstances that might lead to a European role in Southwest Asia, but offers some examples to illustrate that the opportunities for warfare in the region remain. The Iran-Iraq conflict is not fully resolved, despite the fact that the two states have some basis for cooperation in their mutual hostility toward the West. The Kurdish insurgencies and paramilitary activities in Syria, Turkey, Iran, and Iraq could conceivably precipitate wider violence. In the Gulf Arab states, charges of "rentier politics" and a small but growing number of people who are alienated from their regimes may eventually produce violence. Territorial disputes also contribute to regional tensions, with Iran, Iraq, Syria, Kuwait, Yemen, the United Arab Emirates, and Jordan facing claims on portions of their territory from multiple claimants. Regional arms races, disputes between Islamic sects over care of the holy cities or some other issue, Ba'athist resurgence, oil-based arguments, and Turkish-Iranian competition for influence among Turkic peoples of the former Soviet Union represent some of the issues with the potential to produce significant future violence. Most of these could endanger the flow of oil and prompt a Western response.[1]

Strategy will play a central role in the region's military dimensions. All states in the region appreciate the need to have enough military capabilities (either their own or their allies') to discourage their neighbors from acting against them and to defend themselves in the event they face a regional aggressor. Furthermore, the Gulf War impressed everyone in the region with the level of Western military capability. As a result, the non-status-quo states will undoubtedly try to limit Western influence and presence. More important, they have learned that they cannot challenge Western military might directly in a force-on-force contest; they must instead develop asymmetrical strategies if they are to prevail.[2]

What constitutes an asymmetrical strategy? Here the term means any approach that precludes the Western forces from fighting in their preferred modes or that keeps the Europeans from bringing their forces to bear effectively against the enemy. In addition, the term implies that the adversary will undertake effective, unexpected actions against the European forces for which there are few or limited countermeasures. The asymmetrical strategy thus avoids European military strengths and strikes at its weaknesses. The elements of such a strategy in Southwest Asia might involve:

- Disrupting the deployment of European forces to reduce the combat power that eventually reaches the region,

- Intimidating other states in the region to deprive Europe of local bases and a host nation,

---

[1]For a more thorough treatment of the issue, see Robert O. Freedman (ed.), *The Middle East After Iraq's Invasion of Kuwait* (Gainesville: University Press of Florida, 1994).

[2]Many asymmetrical strategies are possible, of course. See Bruce W. Bennett, S. Gardiner, D. Fox, and N. K. J. Witney, *Theater Analysis and Modeling in an Era of Uncertainty: The Present and Future of Warfare*, (Santa Monica, Calif.: RAND, MR-380-NA, 1994).

- Destroying the enemy's advantage in tactical mobility,

- Threatening the expeditionary force's lines of supply and communication in theater and with Europe,

- Inflicting maximum casualties on Western forces without accepting direct combat,

- Avoiding traditional military engagements and preserving combat power,

- Disrupting the European domestic scene, inciting unrest in the Moslem immigrant community through underground resistance and anti-Western propaganda, and threatening direct retaliation against Europe, and

- Preventing formation of an organized coalition of European states.

Such a strategy, if successful, would confront the European allies with circumstances in which their adversary endures, they risk punitive strikes at home, their operations in the region are protracted and costly, and there is no victory on the horizon. The strategy expects the collapse of either the domestic political will or the military capability of the invading Westerners.

Military capabilities in the region, the third factor for consideration, have been growing steadily since Desert Storm, except for Iraq. Most of the regional states have significant acquisition programs. Some have coproduction agreements with suppliers from outside the region, and some are self-sufficient in certain classes of armaments, typically small arms.

Iran

Table 3 summarizes the major weapons and forces that might be at Tehran's disposal in the near term. Iran, perhaps the leading non-status-quo state, has undertaken a major military reform. Tehran is reorganizing its general-purpose forces to make a smaller, more professional military instrument. Despite its reduced oil revenues, Iran has made a significant investment in military spending as it seeks to replace its aging inventory of U.S.-supplied arms with newer equipment secured from Russia, Ukraine, China, and elsewhere. The

Table 3

Iranian Conventional Arms

Tanks	800
AIFV/APCs	680
Artillery	749
Attack helicopters	10
Combat aircraft	178

SOURCES: USNI Database *Periscope*, 20 January 1994; Shlomo Gazit (ed.), *The Middle East Military Balance 1992–93*, pp. 234–249.

NOTE: Tank holdings are disputed. Some sources attribute 700–800, while others estimate as many as 1650. AIFV = armored infantry fighting vehicle.

role and influence of the Pasdaran (Revolutionary Guard forces) have been attenuated somewhat, although these units have not been fully integrated with the regular armed forces and still constitute a competing source of military power.[3]

As Table 3 suggests, Iran could preside over a fairly modern force built principally from arms available on the international export market.[4] If Tehran continues to pursue its current policies, the force would contain some 12 army divisions, small but proportionate air forces, and supporting air defenses. The army could have five armor divisions, five mechanized divisions, and two infantry—perhaps air-mobile—divisions. The air force could have small fighter/attack squadrons to support the army divisions and an air defense/intercept squadron. Tehran appears to be pursuing all available sources in its attempt to acquire appropriate army and air force weapons systems. The national air defense network is outdated, and Tehran has been aggressive in trying to modernize it. Thus far, the military has succeeded in securing some Russian and Chinese surface-to-air missile (SAMs), principally SA-2, SA-5, and SA-10. An air surveillance

---

[3]Anoushiravan Ehteshami, "Iran's National Strategy," *International Defense Review*, April 1994, pp. 29–37, and Andrew Rothmell, "Iran's Rearmament—How Great a Threat?" *Jane's Intelligence Review*, July 1994, pp. 317–322.

[4]This is, however, highly contingent upon Tehran's ability to develop a reliable logistics system and to secure the replacements and spare parts to feed it.

system has been more elusive, although Iran has been negotiating with a Czech firm to acquire a Tamara system allegedly capable of detecting stealth aircraft.

Pasdaran forces would continue to be deployed on an area basis for internal security, surveillance along selected borders, and vigilance against counterrevolutionary activity. Although these forces have undergone some modernization and deploy some armor and mechanized formations accompanied by an air support element, they have only recently organized along traditional military lines, adopted the use of military rank, and similar advancements. At best they represent large paramilitary forces; at worst, an armed rabble.

The military order of battle, by itself, does not offer adequate insights into the state's true capabilities. Questions as to how these equipment and formations are employed—the relevant doctrine, strategy, tactics, and command and control practices—are central to any operational assessment. For example, are maneuver elements supported by reconnaissance and intelligence assets adequate to help them maneuver against an adversary? Is command and control sufficiently agile and responsive to issue appropriate and timely orders? Is coordination among the various maneuver and fire support arms adequate to provide for combined arms operations? Finally, given the lack of professionalism demonstrated during the Iran-Iraq war, has Iranian military science advanced to a point where the armed forces can function in a modern military fashion?

Tehran enjoys some reconnaissance and intelligence capabilities that could be exploited to significant advantage. Its cooperative effort with France to obtain a telecommunications satellite might be suggestive of other space-based capabilities for reconnaissance and surveillance. Tehran might make use of the SPOT commercial satellite, but would in all likelihood be denied its output in any confrontation involving European forces. The Iranian aircraft inventory includes electronic warfare and surveillance and maritime patrol planes. Iran has been seeking airborne early warning (AEW) and airborne warning and control system capabilities and may be acquiring IL-A-50 AEW/AWACS. Even if these negotiations fail, opportunities through other purveyors will in all likelihood produce this capability within a few years. The Iranian army has enough special forces to provide each corps headquarters with a brigade of these troops.

Apportioned carefully throughout the corps force structure, these special forces could provide a valuable source of reconnaissance and battlefield intelligence.

On balance, however, Tehran's reconnaissance and intelligence capabilities will probably remain marginal. Even if the current acquisition plans reach fulfillment, the military will not be adequately equipped to monitor the amount of terrain and the multiple approaches into Iranian territory for which they are responsible. No clear information is available to determine what and how many tactical intelligence systems the military might be buying, but the near-term concentration on reconstituting primary combat systems (e.g., tanks, artillery, armored personnel carriers) suggests that, if there is an acquisition effort directed toward ground surveillance radars and signals intelligence gathering, it has a low priority.

The next index of Tehran's real military capability—the agility of its command and control—suggests that military capabilities have been subordinated to other factors more important to the Islamic Republic. That is, the dysfunctions observed during the Iran-Iraq war—rigidity and hierarchical organization incapable of speedy decisions—have not been corrected despite attempts to streamline the chain of command. Issues of regime survival continue to dominate and place personal loyalty and dependability above military competence. As a result, command and control remain structurally cumbersome and pervaded with officers of solid reliability but questionable military skills. These shortcomings are likely to endure as long as the regime.

The third measure of military capability, the ability to conduct combined-arms operations, remains more open to question. At present, little progress has been made beyond the levels of incompetence demonstrated during the war with Iraq. Field artillery continues to deliver mostly unobserved fires. There seems to be little coordination between maneuver and fire support (indeed, one wonders how much there might be to coordinate if the artillery cannot adjust fire in synchronization with maneuver). Recent combined-arms exercises have been principally naval, coordinating surface and air arms. Some exercises included a limited role for marines. Nevertheless, these shortfalls might be overcome with training support—support that the military receives in the form of advice and instruction from several countries, including North Korea, China, Pakistan, and Russia. In addition, Tehran sends military students to France, North Korea, and Pakistan. However, encumbered by the command and control impediments noted above, by erratic procurement practices that have yielded an incoherent mix of equipment and doctrine, and by the fact that training remains anathema to the forces, it seems doubtful that a modern combined-arms capability will emerge in the immediate future.

The final factor considered here that bears on Iran's net military capabilities is professionalism. The military has sought to reform its service schools to provide a higher caliber of training, but so far has enjoyed little success. For all the reasons noted above, there is little basis to expect that the Islamic Republic's forces are becoming more professional. In addition, the education system in Iran does not support the Western notion of professionalism or provide the skills necessary to sustain a professional military.

Despite their attempts to modernize, the Iranian armed forces remain crippled by a lack of professionalism that limits the military's ability to repair its nonfunctional logistics system or to master the basics of combined-arms warfare. The damage to the education system since the advent of the Islamic Republic and the attendant isolation from the Western military establishment have deprived not only the military but Persian society at large of the skills necessary to move into the next century. Based upon these developments, it seems unlikely that Tehran will have a capable general-purpose military force at its disposal in the near term, no matter what specific weapons and equipment the Iranian military buys.

Having concluded that Tehran will not command very capable conventional forces in the years immediately ahead, it remains to examine what alternative approach—asymmetrical strategy—the regime might invent to stave off European expeditionary forces. As Table 4 suggests, Iran enjoys some means that could support an unconventional defense: its navy and in particular its submarines, its surface-to-surface missiles (SSMs), its naval and land mines, and its nuclear and biological weapons. These assets are less likely to fall prey to the weaknesses attributed to the conventional forces if they are employed in a way that does not place a premium on professional military capabilities. For example, evidence of submarine patrols in

Table 4

Iranian Assets for an Asymmetrical Strategy

Nuclear weapons	2 × 40 kT Scud C warheads
	1 × 50 kT air-deliverable device
	unk × kT artillery projectile
	10 × unk NoDong 1 warheads
Biological weapons	Capability for covert employment
	50–100 × Scud B warheads
Surface-to-surface missiles	300+ × Scud B
	100+ × Scud C
	20–40 × NoDong 1
	300+ × Silkworm
	unk × Iran 130/200
	unk × Mushak 130/160/200
	unk × Scorpion
	unk × Sunburn
Submarines	4 × Kilo class
	2 × Iranian midget
	1 × North Korean midget
Mines	1800 × sea mines
	unk × EM52 rocket-powered mines

SOURCES: Barbara Starr, "NoDongs may soon be nuclear warns USN," *Janes Defense Weekly*, Vol. 21, No. 24, 18 June 1994, p. 1; USNI Database *Periscope*, 20 January 1994; Compendium of Proceedings of the Strategic Options Assessments Conference, "Counter-Proliferation: Deterring Emerging Nuclear Actors," 7–8 July 1993, Strategic Planning International, Inc., for the Defense Nuclear Agency, and authors' estimates.

the Gulf of Oman and Arabian Sea, accompanied by Tehran's declaration that it will sink ships guilty of consorting with Iran's enemies, would probably deprive the Europeans of much of their commercial shipping support whether the submarine crews were competent or not. The threat of submarines would be sufficient to prompt insurance companies to direct the fleets they underwrite to stay out of the region. Surface-to-surface missiles (especially those with nuclear or biological warheads) might be maintained under the direct control of the regime, thus obviating the problems of unresponsive command and control and ensuring positive direction over their use, while effectively threatening neighbor states to the point that they would refuse to serve as host nations for the European expeditionary force. Mines likewise demand little of the teams deploying them, but can nevertheless pose a substantial impediment to an expeditionary force's strategic and tactical mobility. Table 4[5] suggests likely Iranian holdings in these critical arms within the next three to five years.

Table 4 deserves elaboration. Some sources, including the U.S. Naval Institute, attribute limited numbers of nuclear weapons to Iran at the present. Other sources, including the National Intelligence Office, have estimated in unclassified fora that Tehran could own warheads within a few years. Trade press coverage of negotiations with North Korea for NoDong missiles suggests that Iran might have a modest, albeit important, inventory in the next few years. Biological weapons are not technically complex, and make a sound adjunct to a nuclear capability. Iran might deploy biological warheads aboard its more plentiful, shorter-range Scuds and reserve its long-range missiles for nuclear delivery. The SSM listings reflect Iran's indigenously produced (with foreign assistance) missiles as well as its imports. Several, the Mushak 160 for example, may become operational in the near term.

Iran might supplement these weapons with other capabilities, enlisting the aid of Libya and radical elements elsewhere to spread unrest within the Islamic immigrant communities of Europe. These populations could be incited to cause riots, disrupt public utilities, and otherwise disturb European domestic life. Although the official figures on immigrant populations are not unusually large, there are sizable concentrations in some cities and officials fear that illegally immigrated members of the Islamic communities may be significantly underestimated—by as many as a million people in Italy, for example. If mobilized, this population might discourage a European

---

[5]The term "asymmetrical strategy" in this and subsequent tables suggests that the weapons and equipment appearing in the table could be arrayed to support an unusual or at least unanticipated approach to warfare. For instance, surface-to-surface missiles, submarines, and mines might be employed to isolate the theater of war and to hold foreign forces at a distance. For a detailed explanation, see John E. Peters, "Technology and Advances in Foreign Military Capabilities," *The Fletcher Forum of World Affairs* (Winter/Spring 1995), pp. 121–131.

operation in Southwest Asia. Popular unrest might be supported by terrorist activities. World Trade Center–like attacks might generate widespread alarm, especially if Iran made clear that subsequent attacks would involve radiological, biological, or nuclear weapons. The prospect of facing radiological, biological, or nuclear contamination at home might give some nations pause and produce new incentives to support a negotiated settlement to the Gulf crisis—whatever its origins.

The final element of such a plan would be the form of resistance once the Europeans arrive. If Iran fought a "people's war" taking advantage of its size, terrain, and the full complement of its irregular and paramilitary forces, it might prove a formidable obstacle. Iran is a country of 636,293 square miles. There are only two states of the former Soviet Union that are larger, Russia and Kazakhstan. It dwarfs Alaska. Much of its interior contains rugged mountains and hill country, and some 20 percent of it is wasteland. If the Pasdaran 300,000-man force were joined by the 120,000 members of the Bassiji militia and the 45,000-member gendarmerie, the regime could wear the expeditionary European force down gradually, in the hope of eventually using the regular Iranian army to deliver the *coup de grace*. The irregulars would rarely stand and fight, preferring to inflict as many casualties as possible on the Westerners and flee (however, it should be noted that the regime has been willing to sustain substantial casualties for a propaganda victory). Periodically, the irregulars might accept battle, but only to serve as bait to draw the Europeans in, allowing the Iranian regular forces to deliver a punishing blow. In addition, to gain leverage over an intruding Western force and to limit the escalation of violence, Iran could hold its large European business community hostage: an act that would not be unprecedented. This approach would require a minimum of military skill or coordination. Furthermore, the terrain is ideal, offering sanctuary to the irregulars if things go wrong. Iranian forces would probably be able to resist indefinitely, inflicting large losses on the Europeans and denying them any prospect of victory.[6]

---

[6]This is essentially the approach employed by the Afghan resistance in its campaign against the Soviets. See Scott R. McMichael, *Stumbling Bear* (New York and London: Brassey's, 1992).

Iran thus constitutes a potentially difficult adversary for any force that opposes it. On one hand, if Tehran attempts a conventional military operation against the allies, the regime may lose its military (and with it the power to rule) to Western forces that are more adroit at modern, high-tempo warfare. On the other hand, if the regime uses its resources creatively, it can confront Europe with the prospect of a miserable, protracted, costly adventure that includes sobering consequences for the European home front.

Iraq

Iraq, another regional predator, has temporarily focused its attention on reorganizing its military forces, reestablishing its domestic military production capabilities, and reorienting its forces for internal security and regime preservation. In the aftermath of its defeat at the hands of coalition forces, Baghdad faced several serious internal challenges, including rebellion in the ranks of the army, a Kurdish revolt, and a series of coup plots. These events prompted Saddam Hussein to undertake his current program. The military has dissolved the Kurdish Militia and Popular Army and reorganized its ground forces around the Republican Guard six division corps. The new force would expand to about 650,000 personnel at full mobilization. The Special Security Organization protects Saddam and Baghdad proper, and runs a domestic intelligence apparatus to secure the regime. Despite reforms, morale in the army is low and mass desertions and surrenders to Kurdish peshmerga forces are not uncommon. The air force, badly mauled in Desert Storm, is also trying to rebuild, but at present commands only a few modern aircraft and faces major obstacles to securing maintenance and spare parts for them. The navy verges on military insignificance. Baghdad's major conventional arms appear in Table 5.

While his military struggles to organize its remaining assets, Saddam Hussein pursues a major rebuilding program. Despite the aerial campaign of Desert Storm, much of Iraq's industrial capacity escaped destruction. Baghdad seeks to reinvigorate and expand this capability to increase its indigenous arms production and to restore its nuclear and chemical weapons programs. As part of this effort, the Ba'athist regime is attempting to reestablish its clandestine arms import network. The CIA estimates that the Iraqi production base

Table 5

Iraqi Conventional Arms

Tanks	2300
AIFV/APCs	4400
Artillery	1200
Attack helicopters	258
Combat aircraft	150

SOURCES: USNI Database *Periscope*, 15 July 1993; Shlomo Gazit (ed.), *The Middle East Military Balance 1992–93*, p. 443.

could yield a nuclear weapon in five to seven years once sanctions are lifted.[7] They might be able to buy a weapon much sooner.

Over the near term of interest in this study, it seems likely that Iraq will continue to concentrate on rebuilding its military power and shoring up the regime's internal security. To some extent, the duration of this phase depends on how long sanctions remain in effect. In addition, the morale problem manifested in the army will require a period of relative peace and calm before any improvement appears; the soldiers are war weary. Until Baghdad secures reliable access to outside supply sources, its reorganization efforts can only advance a limited amount, to the point where the best possible use of residual or seized equipment is made. Thus, an outward-oriented military equipped with modern weapons and capable of modern combined arms operations is highly unlikely in the years immediately ahead.

What about an asymmetrical strategy? Several factors make it more difficult for Baghdad than for Tehran. First, Iraq lacks the SSM inventory and submarines necessary to isolate the region and to impede the Europeans' arrival. Second, Saddam does not enjoy popular support and could not rely on a population armed for a people's war to stand with him (although there is evidence that Saddam is enjoying some success in using the ongoing sanctions and blockade to build anti-Western sentiment and to shore up his regime). Indeed, the lack of loyalty and reliability, in addition to poor

---

[7]USNI database *Periscope*, Iraqi Defense Organization/Strength, 15 July 1993. See also *The Military Balance*, pp. 127–129.

performance during Operation Desert Storm, were important considerations in the decision to stand down the Popular Army and other portions of the force. Moreover, Iraq is a significantly smaller country than Iran. Despite some rough terrain in the east, it is generally open and ill-suited for a people's war. The few remote safe areas already lie in the hands of Kurdish insurgents opposed to the regime.

Of course, some elements of an unconventional strategy remain at Saddam's disposal. Iraq could still underwrite terrorism or incite immigrant populations against their European hosts. Baghdad could take significant countermobility steps with a strategic mining campaign. Nevertheless, it seems doubtful Saddam would embrace the risk involved. Until he is able to reconstitute his armed forces and domestic arsenal, his regime remains especially vulnerable. Saddam's power is secured by the Special Security Organization, a relatively small and vulnerable force. These units might be specifically targeted by an expeditionary forces with the explicit objective of toppling the Baghdad government. If Saddam Hussein recognizes the tenuous condition of his rule, he is unlikely to confront any European force in the region, by either conventional or unconventional means.

Syria

Syria is perhaps the most militarily capable non-status-quo state in the region. It enjoyed a military relationship with the Soviet Union that, until 1989, provided Syria some of the most advanced equipment in the Soviet arsenal. In addition to its army of five armored divisions, three mechanized divisions and supporting units, Damascus deploys an 1800-man Desert Guard opposite Iraq, a 14,000-man independent Special Force for counterinsurgency along its borders, and an 8000-man gendarmerie for domestic defense.[8] The Syrian army acquitted itself well against Iraq in Desert Storm and severely damaged the forces of General Auon in Lebanon. The army has been engaged in the Lebanese civil war for years and has drawn important lessons in urban combat and guerrilla warfare from

---

[8]USNI Database *Periscope*, 28 April 1992. See also *The Military Balance*, pp. 139, 140.

its experience there. As a result, Syria represents one of the two most able Arab armies (the other being Egypt). The air force deploys nine fighter/ground attack squadrons and 17 air defense/intercept squadrons. It enjoys some of the most advanced Soviet aircraft, and over half of Damascus' combat aircraft inventory are top of the line. In addition to its combat role, the air force also provides border patrol in desert areas unsuitable for ground troops. The navy is small, with three Romeo-class submarines, one of which is thought to be fully operational. The navy deploys about 24 fast attack and patrol craft, two frigates, a fleet of 10 mine warfare ships, and some 20 anti-submarine helicopters. An estimate of Syrian conventional arms appears in Table 6.

Damascus has been cooperating with Iran on missile development and joint production of a nuclear device. Syria has been the recipient of advanced Scud-B and C missiles from North Korea and expects to receive the NoDong missile from Pyongyang as well as the M-9 missile from China. Damascus is thought to have both a chemical and biological weapon capability. [9] Table 7 estimates Syrian arms for an asymmetrical strategy.

How might Damascus employ its conventional military capability to thwart unwanted European activity in the region? It might cooperate with Iran in isolating the area. While Iran dominated the Persian Gulf, Syria could watch and try to interdict the Mediterranean approaches. Moreover, given that Damascus has long sought to or-

Table 6

Syrian Conventional Arms

Tanks	4800
AIFV/APCs	4980
Artillery	2400
Attack helicopters	100
Combat aircraft	532

SOURCES: USNI Database *Periscope,* 28 April 1992; Shlomo Gazit (ed.), *The Middle East Military Balance 1992–93,* pp. 387–389.

---

[9]See fn. 8; see also *Middle East Military Balance,* p. 389.

Table 7

Syrian Assets for an Asymmetrical Strategy

Nuclear weapons	unk × air-deliverable device
	1–3 × unk NoDong 1 warheads
	Possible warheads for Scuds and their derivatives
Biological weapons	Capability for covert employment
	~54 × Scud/variant missile warheads
Surface-to-surface missiles	54 × Frog 7
	54 × SS-21
	54 × Scud B
	12 × Scud C
	unk × NoDong 1
	54 × M-9
Submarines	1 × Romeo class

SOURCES: USNI Database *Periscope,* 28 April 1992; *Middle East Military Balance,* IISS, *The Military Balance 1993–94*; and authors' estimates.

NOTE: SSM estimates derived from assuming three missiles per reported launcher.

chestrate collective Arab activity (it tried to organize an Arab coalition against Iraq after it invaded Kuwait), the Assad regime might try to organize resistance to an expeditionary force by enlisting Libyan and perhaps Algerian support in addition to that of Iran. Even the prospect of a more limited Syrian-Iranian coalition with nuclear and biological weapons might prove a daunting one, given Damascus' modern conventional arsenal and the size of Tehran's force. Of course, Hafez al Assad watched Iraq's fate unfold on CNN during the Gulf War. He also remembers Syria's loss of the Golan Heights to Israel. Moreover, the Syrian battle with Baghdad's forces during Desert Storm was principally an artillery duel and hardly stands as a clear measure of Damascus' military superiority. Assad may, therefore, have doubts about the net military prowess at his disposal. For all these reasons, unless Syria succeeds in recruiting broad-based Arab support, Assad is unlikely to confront a European force directly.

The prospects of an asymmetrical approach are somewhat better. Although Syria lacks the submarines and mines to impede shipping in the eastern Mediterranean on its own, it might enlist Libyan aid to supplement Damascus' meager resources. Libya's Qaddafi has long seen himself as supplier to his Arab brothers in their task of fending off the West. He bought more military equipment than Libya could ever use just to stockpile it for others. As was the case with Iran, Syria might incite domestic unrest in Europe or use terrorism to discourage or punish European adventures in the region. Syria could use its nuclear, biological, and chemical weapons to intimidate moderate states into passivity, depriving European forces of local host-nation basing and support. In addition, its years of experience in Lebanon equip Syrian forces for protracted guerrilla warfare. Although Syrian terrain is not as vast as that of Iran and a Syrian unconventional campaign would therefore be somewhat more vulnerable, the Assad regime might nevertheless be able to fulfill the criteria for a successful asymmetrical campaign, inflicting enough damage on the enemy over an extended period of time while preserving its own forces, leading the foe eventually to demoralization and withdrawal.

The Southwest Asia of the near future will be significantly different from that of 1991. The advent of nuclear weapons is clearly the most dangerous event, with the greatest potential to threaten an expeditionary force with disaster. Biological weapons offer similar though distinct dangers, since it may be possible to launch an attack that is so stealthy that the victim does not recognize either the assault or the adversary—thus making both protective measures and retaliation nearly impossible. The threat of nuclear and biological attack may make sea basing for the expeditionary force mandatory. As noted, few nations will offer the use of their facilities to the West if the invitation makes them vulnerable to these kinds of weapons. Sea basing may also afford the expeditionary force greater protection from nuclear and biological attacks, especially if some of the ships deploy anti-missile defenses.

But the seas, too, will be more dangerous. Submarines, advanced mines, shore-based missiles, and anti-ship helicopters can increase the stand-off distance from the coast ships must maintain to be secure. This means shorter-range carrier aircraft have less use, fewer sorties can be generated, and all forces face a longer, more dangerous trip to the beach. Indeed, the journey from Europe may become more hazardous if inventive adversaries begin interdiction operations in the central Mediterranean—or in European railroad yards.

More than before, the states of Southwest Asia need not allow their enemies an unencumbered approach into the theater. Several actors in the region control the means to begin the military confrontation in Europe. It is conceivable that a force deploying from Europe will risk significant damage en route. Furthermore, it may have to force its way ashore, secure a lodgment area, and protect itself from nuclear and conventional attacks concurrent with its arrival.

EUROPEAN MILITARY COOPERATION

Chapter Three presented a notion of the dangers in Southwest Asia awaiting any incursion from the West; Chapter Four examines the European states and their capability for cooperative military activity. This examination involves several steps. First, the political basis for cooperation will affect any prospects for cooperation among the NATO states and among the wider European community of nations. Second, it is important to determine what minimum, essential capabilities any task force must have to be successful against an adversary in Southwest Asia. Finally, the individual defense programs of European states are examined to gauge the future military resources that may be available for collective action.

The states of Europe have not yet agreed on a comprehensive security architecture.[1] The roles and relations among regional entities, including NATO, WEU, the Conference on Security and Cooperation in Europe (CSCE), and others, have yet to be rationalized, and relations between European organizations and the UN remain convoluted and inchoate. Disagreements on basic approaches to security persist, creating conditions ripe for strategic paralysis in which a looming crisis might be considered successively by several different bodies without producing any concrete action. In the absence of the long-sought security architecture, Europe must build *ad hoc* coalitions of the willing to deal with future crises.

---

[1]For a concise summary of the state of events, see Werner J. Feld, *The Future of European Security and Defense Policy* (Boulder, Colo.: Lynne Rienner Publishers, 1993).

The ability to craft such collaborative efforts is contingent in part upon the nature of the crisis. There is consensus among its members (and perhaps among some of the states engaged in the Partnership for Peace) that NATO remains the instrument for national and Alliance defense. There is also widely held agreement to the Petersberg Declaration as the basis for rescues, humanitarian assistance, and peace operations. There is very little agreement on military activities that fall somewhere between national defense and peace operations and involve the prospect of combat. However, stability missions and similar operations other than war (OOTW) may draw participants from several states. These activities may be viewed as especially attractive missions in non-NATO capitals as a means to demonstrate worthiness for membership in the Alliance and to develop closer ties with the member states. Operations that are expected to involve sustained combat or that include the risk of nuclear or biological weapons attack may attract far fewer participants. Indeed, many Europeans continue to conceive of their security in narrow terms and are unwilling to face sustained combat except in instances of direct self-defense.

Despite recent rulings by the German Constitutional Court that German armed forces could be employed beyond German territory with the approval of the parliament, it is not clear that the *Bundestag* would give its blessing to an operation that would put German troops in harm's way. That is, while Germany would probably be prepared to participate in a peace operation, the prospect of Desert Storm–like combat might be beyond Berlin's threshold of acceptable risk. New German security concepts, discussed briefly in Chapter Five, suggest that this is the case. Other states face similar constraints. Although many European forces plan to phase out conscription in the near term, it remains an impediment to out-of-area activity for some since these states typically have prohibitions against the use of draftees outside the national territory unless they volunteer for it. While some countries have managed the conscript issue easily (France, for example, learning from its Gulf War experience, includes only volunteers and professionals in its *Force d'Action Rapide*), conscripts will continue to limit the forces that can be generated by some states for contingencies such as any in Southwest Asia.

Thus, coalitions of the willing—especially for the more daunting missions—may include few participants. In Desert Storm, where a sizable proportion of Europe's oil supply was at risk and where the foe was clearly engaged in trying to improve its military prowess and strategic reach, only Britain, France, and Italy provided combat forces.[2] Other states were content with a more limited, supporting role. If future contingencies pose similar threats, European participation may prove equally limited.[3]

Assuming that there will be a European military response to a crisis in Southwest Asia, what must the Europeans be able to do to achieve their military objectives? That is, what are the minimum, essential capabilities that the Europeans must have in their military repertoires regardless of the specifics of a given crisis? Based upon the foregoing discussion of the options available to their antagonists and the nature of the region, six key tasks seem to be part of any European response to trouble in Southwest Asia. The Europeans must be able to maintain peace at home; move forces to the theater of operations; establish bases there; protect their forces from nuclear, biological, and chemical attack; win a traditional, force-on-force battle; and contain a people's war.

Domestic security may not be easy to guarantee. This threat did not materialize during the Gulf War principally because of aggressive internal security practices, especially in Italy and France. Things might turn out differently if a Middle Eastern adversary deliberately developed the ability to strike from within Europe or if immigrant populations grow larger and more dissatisfied with life in the West. In such circumstances, civil unrest in support of the Southwest Asian adversary could be substantial, especially among large, restive Moslem populations of uneducated, poor workers who are prone to extreme emotionalism about their faith, especially where *jihad* can be plausibly invoked.[4] Moreover, small numbers of committed terrorists can be very disruptive, as the activities of the Irish Republican Army, Black September, the Red Army Faction, and similar groups

---

[2]Others deployed combat aircraft to Turkey as part of NATO's Allied Mobile Force (Air), but none saw combat.

[3]Europe's response to Iraq during the autumn of 1994 bears out this point. Only Britain and France made a military response.

[4]France, for example, has approximately 5.5 million such residents. See Ian O. Lesser, *Mediterranean Security: New Perspectives and Implications for U.S. Policy* (Santa Monica, Calif.: RAND, R-4178-AF, 1992) p. 48.

have demonstrated in recent years.[5] Add to terrorist activity mass demonstrations, riots, and civil disobedience in cities containing major ports or railroad yards essential to the military effort, and the requirements to maintain public order could become quite demanding. Countries that seek to secure the peace at home in the face of such threats must be able to take precautionary measures against terrorism. This means they must have a domestic intelligence apparatus that warns of impending attacks and helps to identify the perpetrators. States must have counterterrorist forces that can preempt and respond to terrorist activities. They must also have adequate internal security and paramilitary forces to secure key utilities and facilities and to quell public disturbances.

A deployment to Southwest Asia would be a massive, complicated undertaking. During the first 30 days of Desert Shield, for example, the United States moved 123,590 tons of cargo via surface shipping and an additional 39,991 tons through airlift. About 38,000 troops deployed by air as well.[6] Only Britain and France have the means to conduct a strategic deployment, and their assets are extremely limited.[7] Whatever arrangements the Europeans find to move their forces to the theater, they must also be able to protect the ports that they intend to use for debarkation. Since the majority of shipping available to the Europeans will be commercial and non-Ro-Ro, the coalition will be dependent upon port facilities, especially cranes, to unload conventional cargo ships. The Europeans must therefore be able to protect the local dock workers and the cranes. Sabotage of a few cranes and other material-handling equipment, or a chemical or biological attack against the stevedores, could have disastrous results for the European component of any expedition.

---

[5]See K. Gardela and B. R. Hoffman, *RAND Chronology of International Terrorism for 1986* (Santa Monica, Calif.: RAND, R-3890-RC, 1990) and W. W. Fowler, *Terrorism Database: A Comparison of Missions, Methods, and Systems* (Santa Monica, Calif.: RAND, N-1503-RC, 1981).

[6]Lieutenant General William G. Pagonis with Jeffrey L. Cruikshank, *Moving Mountains: Lessons in Leadership and Logistics from the Gulf War* (Boston, Mass.: Harvard Business School Press, 1992), pp. 1–7.

[7]To get its modest expeditionary force to the Falklands, for example, Britain had to charter commercial shipping. Much of its heavy equipment deployed on seagoing tugs and barges taken from their English Channel routes. The French own five LPDs and a small fleet of Ro-Ro ships. However, these assets are inadequate to transport the divisions of the *Force d'Action Rapide* (FAR).

Establishing basing is the next task. If the expedition is to enjoy regional support, it must be able to convince the relevant countries that it can protect them from NBC attack—possibly by extending air defense and theater missile defense to cover critical facilities belonging to their local hosts. If the Europeans fail to win regional support, they may be faced with the prospect of forcing entry into the theater and protecting their lodgment until they can reinforce. A forced-entry operation would have major implications for the success of the European expedition. If the Europeans do not possess the capability to force their way ashore against a determined defender, they would have to find an area that was at best lightly defended in which to land and then make an approach march into the area of operations. If the coalition succeeds in establishing a lodgment, it will probably require a much larger force to operate safely in the presence of a hostile population, since the expeditionary force will now have to secure all of its facilities—its logistics bases, camps, and lines of communication. Thus, acquiring the willing support of a local nation is essential to keeping coalition force requirements proportionate with what the Europeans might be able to generate.

One task that pervades all others is the need to protect the force against air and missile attack. A catastrophic loss brought about because the enemy saturated the Europeans' defenses and successfully delivered a single nuclear weapon might cause the coalition to fracture and abandon its mission. The Europeans would have to discourage any NBC attack against their expedition and at the same time erect concentric spheres of defense that would defeat air and missile attacks. At the innermost sphere, the expeditionary force would have to prepare its troops, providing vaccinations and pretreatments against the toxins and agents that might be used, training the soldiers and airmen to perform their tasks while wearing protective equipment, and providing protective masks, suits, and filters in sufficient quantities that personnel could decontaminate each other and still protect themselves from subsequent attacks. The next sphere of protection would provide terminal defenses against attackers who manage to reach the expeditionary force units. This arc of defense would have to be capable of destroying cruise and ballistic missiles and aircraft. It would also have to locate and destroy artillery capable of firing NBC projectiles. Finally, the outer sphere would have to orchestrate active and passive defenses with offensive counterair and "Scud hunting" operations to produce the overarching defensive layer. This tier of protection would seek out and destroy enemy aircraft and missile launchers at their airfields and assembly areas.

Defeating the enemy is certainly among the most complicated tasks any expeditionary force will have to complete. Many different strategies are possible, but most either are centered on the enemy force, seeking to destroy it or compel its surrender, or focus on destruction of the regime's praetorian guard forces, thus leaving the leadership vulnerable and its fate in the hands of the coalition. A third general approach, concentrating on the immiseration of the populace and trying to spawn a rebellion, seems an improbable strategy because the European polity would be unwilling to break the laws of warfare as the scheme requires and because the Western expeditionary force would still have to deal with the enemy military even though the population arose against the regime.

Both of the general approaches envisioned here involve destroying large portions of the enemy forces. This process requires the ability to locate enemy formations, to engage individual units, to destroy these units to a degree that they cease to offer organized resistance, and to conduct stability operations and impose order once a cease-fire is concluded. To succeed, a coalition would have to reconnoiter the depth of the battle space and to locate and engage the enemy early, before he can bring forces to bear. The reconnaissance could be performed by some combination of troops, aerial surveillance, and the technical intelligence collection disciplines. Engaging the enemy would involve air and ground attacks. If the expedition is to avoid a tank-to-tank *Schlagfest,* the Europeans will need the means to blind the enemy and deprive him of crucial information about the locations and intentions of friendly forces. Air forces will require suppression of enemy air defenses and stand-off weapons if they are to attack deep targets. Without the participation of U.S. forces, a European coalition deployed to the region in the next few years would lack certain reconnaissance, intelligence, surveillance, target acquisition, electronic warfare, and suppression of enemy air defense (SEAD) capabilities necessary to prevail without sustaining heavy casualties.

Containing a people's war generally involves an extended stability operation. Stability operations, to be successful, must achieve certain ratios of troops per thousand members of the populace. This is not to say that merely achieving a certain level of presence will produce success; it will not. But an otherwise satisfactory approach, if undermanned, cannot succeed. The ongoing British operation in Ulster requires a presence of approximately 20 security personnel per thousand people, the recent Somalia mission about four per thousand. It is therefore somewhat conservative to suggest that a European expeditionary force might require on the order of four to six troops per thousand to confine such a conflict to an acceptable level of violence. Without the participation of U.S. forces, a Western coalition would have trouble sustaining the required presence over a protracted period. The small size of their professional forces means that they lack the depth to provide a rotation base.

Chapter Five

NATIONAL CAPABILITIES

This chapter examines the individual military programs of the 14 European NATO members and selected Central European states. The NATO states tend to organize their forces according to the Alliance defense scheme, allocating a majority of their forces as Main Defense Forces, and a much smaller element as Reaction Forces.[1] They generally rely upon the Alliance for national and collective defense, and envision only modest military action abroad, typically peace operations conducted in the context of the 1992 Petersberg Declaration. Most of the Europeans rely more heavily on reserve forces and maintain small active components. Few countries envision employing their forces unilaterally, and most foresee multinational formations as the principal vehicle for military action.[2] Most countries, driven by budgetary considerations, are dramatically reducing their forces. Table 8 provides a rough comparison of national arsenals by showing recent Conventional Forces in Europe treaty equipment declarations for the Europeans along with forecasts of equipment holdings for selected states in Southwest Asia. Of course, with the defense cuts under way across Europe, by 1998 few

---

[1] *North Atlantic Defense and Security Committee 1993 Reports*, AK229 DSC/AF (93)2 (October 1993), Subcommittee on the Future of the Armed Forces Military Trends within the Atlantic Alliance (Brussels: North Atlantic Assembly, 1993) p. 5. Approximately 65 percent of member forces are allocated to Main Defense Forces and 10–15 percent to Reaction Forces.

[2] For example, a division comprised of Greek, Italian, and Turkish units with its headquarters in Salonika is intended as a Balkan and eastern Mediterranean intervention force, according to Andrew Borowiec, "New NATO intervention force planned for Balkans," *Washington Times*, September 21, 1994, p. 10.

Table 8

Force Comparisons

Equipment	BE	CZ	DK	F	GE	GR	HU	IT	NL
Tanks	339	1525	452	1309	5498	2458	1191	1354	740
Armored combat vehicles	985	2254	273	3964	7155	1453	1645	3402	1195
Artillery	322	1620	553	1429	3504	2063	991	2047	612
Combat aircraft	200	265	101	687	754	495	171	545	173
Attack helicopters	46	36	12	373	250	0	39	166	31

Equipment	NO	PL	PO	SV	SP	TU	UK	Iran	Iraq	Syria
Tanks	262	2515	226	912	1044	3358	958	800	2300	4800
Armored combat vehicles	196	2232	369	1169	1310	1964	2901	680	4400	4890
Artillery	402	2151	354	931	1357	3390	520	749	1200	2400
Combat aircraft	80	446	109	146	174	428	710	178	150	532
Attack helicopters	0	70	0	19	28	35	361	10	258	100

NOTE: BE = Belgium, CZ = Czech Republic, DK = Denmark, F = France, GE = Germany, GR = Greece, HU = Hungary, IT = Italy, NL = Netherlands, NO = Norway, PL = Poland, PO = Portugal, SV = Slovakia, SP = Spain, TU = Turkey, UK = United Kingdom.

states will have military establishments capable of employing all of this equipment. To understand what residual military power will reside in Europe, the defense programs of the individual states must be examined.

Belgium plans a massive reduction in its military—40 to 50 percent of the current forces will be stood down. Under this plan, conscription ends in 1994 and defense will incur a budget ceiling of 98 billion francs by 1997. The active military will include 27,500 troops in the ground forces, 10,000 with the air force, and 2500 with the navy. There are provisions for a reserve, but its size will be determined later. The dimensions of this defense restructuring are so severe that they prompted a letter of opposition from NATO Secretary Manfred Woerner to Belgian Prime Minister Jean-Luc Dehaene in November 1992.[3] Belgium's active ground forces will be reduced to one para-

---

[3] *North Atlantic Defense and Security Committee 1993 Reports*, p. 10.

commando brigade and a 12,000-man mechanized division. The division will be assigned to both NATO and the Eurocorps and the para-commandos will constitute Brussels' contribution to the Allied Command Europe Rapid Reaction Corps (ARRC).

The air forces include four squadrons of ground attack and two squadrons of air defense fighters, both equipped with F-16A/B. A total of 72 aircraft are configured for strike missions and 35 are outfitted for the air defense role. Some 27 additional aircraft remain in storage.[4] The reconnaissance squadron flies 15 Mirage 5-BRs. Modest as these forces are, Belgium lacks the means to deploy them. The navy has no amphibious assault shipping and can provide only two logistic support and command ships. Air transport relies upon 12 C-130s, two HS-748s, and two Boeing 727QCs.

Denmark's military, always of modest size and capability, will become smaller still as major force reductions aim for budget savings of $177 million by the end of 1994. The Danes will rely more heavily on the Home Guard for Main Defense missions. The Jutland Division will be the country's prime contribution to the Atlantic Alliance as part of the LANDJUT Multinational Corps. A 4550-man reaction brigade is planned that will be tasked for NATO rapid reaction corps, CSCE, and UN missions, although it will not be permanently assigned to the ARRC or other international formations. Danish air power is based upon 63 F-16A/B ground-attack and fighter aircraft. A squadron of RF-35 Drakens provides reconnaissance. Like the Belgians, the Danes own no assault shipping and no military air transport fleet.[5]

France, dissatisfied with its capabilities in the Gulf War, is the only European NATO member that plans significant modernization and reorganization to increase its military prowess. Although the army will be reduced from 260,000 to 225,000 troops by 1997, these reductions will be accompanied by a major reorganization of forces and an aggressive acquisition plan. When restructuring is complete, the army will include three armor divisions, two light armor divisions, an airmobile division, one airborne, and one mountain

---

[4]International Institute of Strategic Studies, *The Military Balance 1993–1994* (London: Brassey's, 1993) p. 38.

[5]*North Atlantic Defense and Security Committee 1993 Reports*, pp. 13, 14.

division.[6] Paris intends to increase defense spending by one-half percent annually after inflation to add new equipment, overcome inadequate transportation, and to acquire surveillance and night-vision capabilities.[7] Paris is also improving its ability to command and support distant forces. The army has more than doubled its logistics troops to 45,000 in order to support two and one-third deployed divisions. Communications tests to link French and U.S. strategic communications systems are ongoing and thus far have been successful.[8]

The air force commands 11 squadrons of ground attack aircraft that fly an assortment of 88 Mirages and 117 Jaguars. The four fighter wings fly 98 Mirage F-1C aircraft. The reconnaissance wing deploys over 50 Mirage F-1CRs. The air force also includes two squadrons of electronic warfare aircraft.[9]

The French acquisition plan will provide additional capabilities for the military at large. The M5 ballistic missile, planned for 2002, will provide greater range and accuracy to French prestrategic forces. Twenty Rafael fighters will boost the air force's aging combat air fleet. The army will benefit from the arrival of new attack and support helicopters, as well as delivery of 310 new Leclerc main battle tanks. Paris will also loft two new intelligence satellites and acquire two E-2C Hawkeye surveillance aircraft for the navy. Strategic air transportation will eventually improve with the advent of the Future Large Aircraft (FLA).

Until the FLA becomes reality, France has a modest airlift capability based upon four DC-8Fs, 77 C-160s, and 12 C-130s. The navy pursues a building program that will sustain and improve France's modest force projection capability, providing two aircraft carriers, a helicopter carrier, five underway support ships, 15 transports, and some nine assault ships.[10] Once the new TCD-90 landing ship, dock

---

[6]Ibid, p. 15.

[7]See *Washington Times,* June 13, 1994, p. 14.

[8]Interviews in the French Ministry of Defense, May 4, 1995.

[9]*The Military Balance 1993–1994,* p. 44.

[10]Exact figures for assault shipping depend upon whether the older ships are retired. The navy might deploy as few as five such ships if the oldest are all removed from service. Transport shipping is often augmented by a fleet of six Ro-Ro ships that,

(LSD) enters service in 1997, the navy will be able to embark a mechanized regiment from the FAR with complete logistical, medical, and command facilities. Four of these ships are planned. Each can support 700 troops for 30 days and carry up to 1600 troops in an emergency. Present capabilities are smaller, with the *Ouragon* class able to deploy 340 troops and 11 light tanks.[11]

French aircraft carriers offer a mix of capabilities. The *Charles de Gaulle* is currently under construction, and will be the principal platform for the E-2C Hawkeye aircraft upon its completion in 1999. The carrier is also slated to receive a new air group of 35-40 Rafael SU-2 aircraft. Although not now in the defense plan, a second carrier may be built if economic conditions improve.[12] The *Clemenceau* whose air group could not fly in the Gulf War, may be modernized to support fixed-wing aircraft, or may be relegated to duty as a helicopter carrier (CVH) or helicopter assault ship (LPH). The current CVH can support 12 helicopters.

Near-term German defense planning[13] remains dominated by an acquisition freeze and budget cuts, with another 20 percent reduction foreseen by 1996. The army, according to the *Konzept des Bundesministers der Verteidigung zur Stationierungsplanung der Bundeswehr*, is tasked to defend German borders, support NATO flanks in Norway and Turkey, and be prepared for international tasks within the constitutional framework. To this end, it will have seven fully active brigades, including one mountain, three mechanized infantry, and two airmobile brigades, as well as its elements in the Franco-German brigade. Eighteen mechanized brigades will be partially active units, as will one airmobile brigade. Two cadre-

---

although commercial, habitually support French forces. See Frances Tusa, "France's Forces from the Sea: Interview with Maj. Gen. Tanneguy Le Pichon, Commander of France's 9th DIMA," *Armed Forces Journal International,* September 1994, p. 15.

[11]Captain Richard Sharpe RN (ed.), *Jane's Fighting Ships 1994–95* (London: Butler and Tanner Ltd., 1994), p. 219.

[12]*Washington Times,* 13 June 1994, p. 14.

[13]The narrow margin of victory for Helmut Kohl's CDU/FDP coalition in the 16, October 1994 Federal German elections adds a new degree of uncertainty to German defense planning. Contrary-minded members of the opposition in the *Bundestag* now stand a better chance of undermining the government's defense program. The description of the German military in this chapter anticipates that the government will succeed in pursuing its defense plans.

strength brigades complete the force structure. When the reductions throughout the German military are complete, the *Bundeswehr* will contain only half the units it possessed in 1990. [14]

Most of Germany's forces are associated with the NATO Main Defense Force. When fully reorganized, these will include a U.S.-German corps and a Netherlands-German corps. During peacetime, the U.S.-German corps will maintain only a planning staff. Its sister corps will also be a low-readiness unit.[15] General Klaus Naumann, Chief of Defense Staff, has directed the army to earmark one division for deployment outside of NATO. He also directed the air force to prepare air transport for this formation.[16] Despite General Naumann's instructions to ready expeditionary forces, the emerging concepts of "defense at distance" and "Germany as COMMZ" (the theater rear) of Europe suggest that Germany remains unprepared politically for operations that include significant risk of combat other than national defense. Under these two notions, Germany would hold the center of Europe, providing deterrence and reassurance while France and Britain respond to crises on the flanks.[17]

German air power resides in a fleet of Tornado aircraft supplemented by aging Phantom F-4s. Between the air force and navy, Germany deploys nine attack squadrons containing some 240 Tornado air-craft, and one squadron of F-4Fs. Air defense aircraft include one squadron of 20 MiG-29s and six squadrons of F-4Fs. The *Luftwaffe* also employs 43 RF-4E aircraft for reconnaissance.[18]

If defense planning progresses along its current course, by 2005 the army will organize its active brigades into a crisis reaction corps (KRK). The navy may deploy an "all purpose ship" similar to a small helicopter aircraft carrier. The ship will function as a composite

---

[14]Volker Rühe, "Perspektiven deutscher Sircherheitspolitik und Zukunftsaufgaben der Bundeswehr," *Europäische Sicherheit*, January 1994, pp. 9–16. See also AFES Press Report No. 15, Hans Guender Brauch, "The New Europe and Non-Offensive Defense Concepts (Mosbach, 1991).

[15]*North Atlantic Defense and Security Committee 1993 Reports*, pp. 15–17.

[16]Heinz Schulte, "Defence chief outlines leaner Bundeswehr," *Jane's Defence Weekly*, September 10, 1994, p. 15.

[17]Interview in the German Ministry of Defense, May 9, 1995.

[18]*The Military Balance 1993–1994*, p. 48.

troop transport, headquarters, and support ship. It will accommodate 700 troops, light combat vehicles, and six helicopters.[19]

The Italian armed forces are also undergoing reductions, with the army sustaining a 36 percent cut and the air force and navy 20 percent reductions each. The new end strength will include 150,000 active soldiers, 40,000 seamen, and 60,000 airmen. The army will provide five brigades of ready intervention forces for NATO, ultimately around 70,000 troops. The five brigades will comprise a light armor unit, one mechanized, one armor, one alpine, and one *corazzata* (naval) brigade. Rome will also deploy seven or eight brigades of "secondary forces" consisting of five or six mechanized brigades, one *corazzata*, and one alpine. The remainder of Italy's forces will be "category three" reserve units.[20]

Air power resides in nine ground attack squadrons that deploy 66 Tornado, 69 AMX, and 21 G91Y aircraft, six fighter squadrons flying 99 near-obsolete F-104ASA airplanes, and a reconnaissance squadron.[21]

The navy and air force provide modest transport capabilities. Italy deploys two aircraft carriers, each supporting 16 Harriers and 18 helicopters. The fleet also includes three LPDs (landing platforms, dock) capable of transporting 400 troops and 30–36 armored personnel carriers or 30 medium tanks.[22] The air force fields two Boeing 707-320s, 12 C-130s, and 38 G-222 transports.

The armed forces of the Netherlands operate on a budget that has been cut and frozen for the next ten years. Conscription will end in 1998, and the forces will sustain a net reduction of 54 percent of their peacetime strength. By 1998, the army will consist of 23,700 troops, the air force will be 21,000 strong, and the navy about 17,000. The exact form of the reorganization has not been fully established, but

---

[19]USNI Database *Periscope*, Germany Defense Organization and Strength, 3 October 1994. More recently, Defense Minister Rühe has distanced himself from the ship while the navy complains that this ship is expensive and inadequate to sustain operations. See *Der Spiegel*, 8 May 1995.

[20]*North Atlantic Defense and Security Committee 1993 Reports*, p. 17.

[21]*The Military Balance 1993–1994*, p. 52.

[22]Captain Richard Sharpe, RN (ed.), *Jane's Fighting Ships 1994–95* , pp. 327, 328.

there are indicators that the Dutch may lack the forces to contribute their full share to the planned German-Netherlands corps. Indeed, the State Secretary of Defense has invited other countries to contribute to the corps, which might be interpreted as a way to make up the shortfall.[23] Currently, the army deploys four mechanized infantry brigades, one light brigade (two battalions), and one air mobile brigade.

The Netherlands' armed forces have no aircraft carriers or assault shipping and an extremely limited air transportation capability. The air force deploys six C-130 cargo aircraft and three DHC-6s. The F-16A/B constitutes the backbone of Dutch air combat capability. The air force flies 123 of these aircraft organized in eight squadrons and another 19 deployed in a reconnaissance squadron.[24]

Norway maintains its military at a peacetime strength of 20,000 army and 9500 air force troops. Norwegian air forces consist of four F-16 squadrons for ground attack and one fighter and training squadron that flies F-5A/Bs. The army consists of a division and six separate brigades. Oslo's forces are postured primarily for direct defense of the homeland. Norway contributes a battalion battle group to NATO's immediate response forces.[25]

Portugal is pursuing a five-year modernization and reequipping program that will eventually invest $1.1 billion in defense. The army will have a new airborne brigade that should become operational by the end of 1994. Portugal also earmarks a combined-arms brigade for NATO.[26] In addition to these forces, the Portuguese military has three infantry brigades and a light infantry task force. The navy includes three battalions of marines—two infantry and one police battalion. The air force consists of three squadrons flying obsolete A-7Ps and somewhat newer G-91R3s.

---

[23]*North Atlantic Defense and Security Committee 1993 Reports,* p. 20.

[24]*The Military Balance 1993–1994,* p. 54.

[25]*North Atlantic Defense and Security Committee 1993 Reports,* p. 21.

[26]According to the International Institute for Strategic Studies, this brigade includes one mechanized, two motorized, one tank, and one artillery battalion. See *The Military Balance 1993–1994,* p. 57.

The navy and air force have virtually no transport capabilities. The navy owns only an assortment of coastal patrol craft and landing craft, but no assault shipping. The air force deploys 22 C-212 transports and six C-130s, some of which have search-and-rescue missions.

The 1990 Spanish Joint Strategic Plan, like the defense documents of many of its allies, mandated a 14 percent cut in manpower. It did, however, preserve much of Madrid's military capability. Spain arrays its forces in three groupings: the Rapid Action Force, the Maneuver Force, and the Territorial Defense Force. The Rapid Action Force includes a parachute brigade, an infantry regiment, an aviation regiment, and a mountain brigade. These forces are available to the ARRC under special coordination agreements between Madrid and NATO. Spain also provides one brigade to the Eurocorps. The remainder of the Spanish ground forces have Main Defense missions and are unlikely to deploy outside of Spanish territory.

Spain's air forces deploy in four geographically based air commands. Its ground attack aircraft include 22 F-5Bs and 30 Mirage F-1CEs. Fighter squadrons operate 70 EF-18A/B Hornets and a mix of 20 Mirage F-1BE and F-1EE aircraft. Long-range transport is limited to three Boeing 707s, seven C-130s, and 32 C-212 aircraft.

The navy operates one aircraft carrier with a Harrier air group and four assault ships including two amphibious transports capable of deploying 1600 troops and 15 amphibians each. The remaining two transports are LSTs (landing ships, tank), able to accommodate 400 troops and ten tanks each.[27]

Turkey, like many other members of NATO, is reorganizing its armed forces. The army remains the largest of the European members with 370,000 troops, the majority of whom are conscripts. The ground forces include one mechanized and one infantry division, 15 armor brigades, 18 mechanized brigades, nine infantry brigades, and three commando brigades.

The air force consists of 19 ground attack and two fighter squadrons that deploy a mix of mostly older aircraft. Attack missions fall to 126

---

[27] *The Military Balance 1993–1994*, p. 59.

F-16C/D airplanes. Air defense involves some 137 F-5s, 155 F-4s, and 88 F-104s.

Long-range transportation depends upon seven LSTs. Several of these ships are capable of housing up to 600 troops and carrying 16–18 tanks, while others have less capacity, typically providing space for 400 troops and nine tanks. The airlift available is based upon 13 C-130, 19 C-160, and 25 C-47 transports, the latter of World War II vintage.[28]

The United Kingdom plans to reduce defense spending 12 percent over the next five years. According to Chief of Defense Staff Field Marshal Sir Peter Inge, GCB, the center of gravity for the forces is no longer Germany but the UK. Britain will maintain approximately 23,000 people in Germany for the foreseeable future, however.[29] The army will number about 122,000 troops and deploy roughly 40 battalions. Its most significant military capabilities will reside in the ARRC, for which Britain is the "framework nation"—the nation providing the headquarters and most of the combat service support and corps troops. In addition to these, the UK will provide the 3d Mechanized Division, composed of two mechanized and one airborne brigade, and the 24th Air Mobile Brigade to the Multinational Division (Central).[30]

UK air forces contain 13 squadrons of ground attack aircraft, seven fighter squadrons, and two reconnaissance squadrons. The fighter aircraft are modern Tornado F-3s. Almost half of the attack squadrons fly the Tornado GR-1 strike aircraft, but less-capable GR-5 and GR-7 Harriers, Buccaneers, and Jaguars remain in service.

Long-range transportation depends upon the Royal Navy's two aircraft carriers (CVH) and its six amphibious assault ships. The air forces provide 22 VC-10, 13 C-1, and 62 C-130 transports. The carrier air arm deploys Sea Harrier FRS-1 attack planes. The assault shipping includes an LPD capable of transporting 400 troops, 15 tanks,

---

[28] *North Atlantic Defense and Security Committee 1993 Reports*, p. 23. See also *The Military Balance 1993–1994*, p. 61.

[29] Field Marshal Sir Peter Inge, GCB, "The Capability Based Army," *RUSI Journal*, Vol. 139, No. 3 (June 1994), pp. 1–5.

[30] Ibid. See also *North Atlantic Defense and Security Committee 1993 Reports*, p. 23.

and three helicopters; and five LSTs, each capable of carrying 340 troops and from 16 to 18 tanks, plus a helicopter. The army also owns a fleet of assorted landing craft and tugs, some of which served in the Falklands campaign.[31]

Despite defense reductions, some modernization will occur. The army will receive 259 new Challenger II tanks and an unspecified number of new attack and support helicopters, as well as advanced anti-armor missiles. The Royal Air Force will upgrade its GR.1 ground attack Tornados to GR.4 standard, take a squadron of Harrier GR.5/7s out of mothballs, and receive the newer Paveway III laser-guided bomb. The navy will replace two of its LPDs, and some sub-marines may be outfitted with Tomahawk conventionally armed land attack missiles.[32] Recent press reports of joint UK-Spanish plans to build new large-deck carriers are premature. In fact, carrier decisions depend upon aircraft developments. If the joint advanced strike (JAST) aircraft develops as planned, the Royal Navy will continue to fly very short take-off and landing (VSTOL) planes and hence will not need large-deck carriers.[33]

Military contributions from Eastern Europe are uncertain at best. Like their Western neighbors, these states seek to adjust their defense postures to the post-Soviet era and broaden their security. Unlike the Western states, however, *Mitteleuropa* lacks the security guarantees of NATO (North Atlantic Cooperation Council and Partnership for Peace notwithstanding) and remains haunted by fears and loyalties from the past. Old fears prompted Poland to complain about the Russian military presence in Kaliningrad Oblast despite the fact that the Russian forces there are within the limits allowed by the Conventional Forces in Europe (CFE) Treaty.[34] Old loyalties prompted Hungary to order NATO AWACS aircraft from Hungarian

---

[31] *The Military Balance 1993–1994*, p. 63. The army is also campaigning for two Ro-Ro ferries, but their acquisition is contingent upon the service's ability to demonstrate the ship's broader utility (interview in United Kingdom Ministry of Defense, May 1, 1995).

[32] Francis Tusa, "A Not-Very-Bitter Pill," *Armed Forces Journal International,* September 1994, pp. 13, 14.

[33] Interview in United Kingdom Ministry of Defense, May 1, 1995.

[34] "Kaliningrad Situation Alarming Poles," *Izvestiya,* 9 April 1994, p. 3, as reported in JPRS-TAC-94-004-L, 22 April 1994, p. 14.

air space when the aircraft were monitoring Bosnia.[35] When combined with the daunting tasks of trying to rebuild their economic and political institutions, the pressures of old fears and loyalties make it difficult to anticipate what, if any, support the East Europeans might provide to future contingency operations.

Hungary typifies the problems confronting these states. The Magyar state is militarily weak, its forces are maldeployed, and it faces territorial claims and ethnic minority issues with virtually all of its neighbors. It is isolated geographically from Western Europe and caught up in the deep sense of mutual suspicion that pervades all of the states in the Danube basin.[36] The Hungarian Defense Forces are small and understrength. As of January 1994, Budapest had about 75,000 personnel under arms, with 41,100 in the army and 18,000 in air defense (missile units and air force squadrons), and over 15,000 in centrally controlled formations composed principally of the national military training establishment, two airlift units, a signal unit, a military police unit, and a combat helicopter regiment.[37]

The Hungarian Defense Forces are organized principally for territorial defense and arrayed in four military districts and an air defense command. The forces in the first, second, and third military districts roughly constitute division equivalents, each deploying at least three maneuver brigades and an assortment of combat support formations: artillery, engineers, and reconnaissance units. Budapest Military District comprises only military police, signal, and engineer units. The backbone of the army seems to be three tank brigades, eight mechanized infantry brigades, three artillery brigades, and an air defense artillery brigade. The air defense command includes three fighter regiments, a SAM brigade, and three SAM regiments,

---

[35]Charles William Maynes, "NATO's Tough Choice in Bosnia," *New York Times*, 27 July 1994, p. 21.

[36]See George Schoepflin, "Hungary and Its Neighbors," Chaillot Paper #7, Institute for West European Studies, Western European Union, May 1993.

[37]Republic of Hungary, "Information on the Conventional Armaments and Equipment and Personnel Strength of the Armed Forces of the Republic of Hungary, valid as of January 1, 1994" (hereinafter, Hungarian CFE annual equipment declaration), 15 December 1993, charts I, IIA, IIB.

plus support units. Air transport capability resides in two An-24, nine An-26, and three L-410 aircraft.[38]

Manning and equipping in units is very uneven. For example, within the first military district, the 31st Mechanized Infantry Brigade fields only 1385 troops, while its sister unit, the 37th Mechanized Infantry Brigade, commands over 2000. Likewise, the 31st Brigade has a complement of 54 tanks, while the 37th Brigade has only 41. Units seem to remain organized along Soviet lines and are therefore somewhat smaller than their western counterparts. A sizable portion of the Hungarian military is understrength.[39]

The equipment throughout the Hungarian Defense Forces is old and reflects the country's Warsaw Pact heritage. All but 138 of the nation's 1191 tanks are obsolete, as are many of its armored personnel carriers and howitzers. The air forces depend upon the MiG-21 for aerial combat power, deploying 117 of this aircraft type (over 40 of these aircraft are in storage). The remainder of the combat air fleet is comprised of small numbers of SU-22s for a surveillance squadron, and MiG-23s and -29s for air defense.[40]

Poland's military suffers from some of the same maladies as Hungary's. The force is weak and maldeployed, largely as a result of its previous role in the Warsaw Pact. Despite Warsaw's candidacy for NATO membership, suspicions abound; Warsaw has fears about its neighbors, including Germany, Russia, Belarus, and Ukraine. At the same time, Belarus is watchful for signs of a Polish-Lithuanian cabal seeking to dominate the region. To mitigate these mutual antagonisms, Poland has enlisted the aid of France to bring stability to the region with the creation of a Franco-German-Polish trio.[41] Unable to determine how its security posture might develop, Poland has opted to redeploy its forces for all-around defense of its territory.

To this end, its ground forces are arrayed in four military districts. Each district has a fairly elaborate system of support facilities and

---

[38]Ibid.

[39]Ibid.

[40]Ibid. See also *The Military Balance 1993–1994,* p. 81.

[41]Valerie Guerin-Sendelbach and Jacek Rulkowski, "'Euro-Trio' Frankreich-Deutschland-Polen," *Aussen Politik,* Jg. 45, 3. Quartal 1994, pp. 246–253.

storage depots, as well as geographically oriented air defenses including SAM or anti-aircraft artillery units. Principal combat formations consist of 10 mechanized infantry and one armored cavalry divisions. The Pomeranian Military District also deploys a coast defense division. These forces are distributed fairly uniformly across Polish territory, with three divisions in the Pomeranian and Warsaw Military Districts, four divisions in the Silesian Military District, and two in the Cracow Military District. The divisions do not share common organizations, however. Instead of the normal three, the 2nd Mechanized Division contains only two regiments and the 9th Mechanized Division only one.[42]

Air forces are organized into an Air Defense Corps and an Air Corps. Ground attack aircraft include 20 SU-20s and 104 SU-22s. Fighters are organized in air defense regiments and deploy 213 MiG-21Us, 37 MiG-23MFs, and 12 MiG-29Us. SAMs, SA-2, -3, and -5 deployed over roughly 50 sites also contribute to air defense.[43]

Long-range transportation resides in two air regiments. The Poles fly an assortment of about 40 Russian-built tactical transports including the An-2, An-12, An-26, YAK-40, and Tu-154. Although the navy owns five *Lubin*-class medium landing craft, each capable of transporting 135 troops and nine tanks, the International Institute for Strategic Studies reports that none of them is employed in an amphibian role.[44]

The Czech Republic is in the midst of an ambitious military reorganization effort that includes a near-term restructuring to make the armed forces more compatible with those of NATO and a long-term modernization program that should come to fruition around 2005, depending upon the state of the economy. By the end of 1995, the logistics system should be compatible with that of NATO. As weapons are modernized, NATO calibers will be adopted.[45]

---

[42]Polish CFE annual equipment declaration 15 December 1993, charts I, IIA, IIB.

[43]Ibid. See also *The Military Balance 1993–1994*, p. 85.

[44]Ibid.

[45]Brigitte Sauerwein, "In Transition: the Army of the Czech Republic," *International Defense Review*, April 1994, pp. 69–71.

By 1996, the military is expected to have a personnel strength of 65,000: a major reduction from the present 106,000. The army will include Field Troops, Rapid Reaction Forces, and Territorial Defense Forces. Field Troops will make up the bulk of seven mechanized brigades planned for 1995. Rapid Reaction Forces, although at present only a battalion strong, will grow to brigade strength by the end of 1995 and be capable of independent operations. Territorial Defense Forces will protect facilities important to the Czech Republic, but their size is uncertain. It is expected that they will be deployed within the current two geographical commands, Military Command Center and Military Command West. Air defenses will include a fighter regiment and four SAM brigades.[46]

Like other former Warsaw Pact members, Prague's military arsenal is comprised of Soviet-era equipment. The Czechs have begun a modernization program for some of their equipment, however, and are upgrading 450 T-72 tanks in cooperation with a French firm. The Czechs are also seeking a wheeled armored personnel carrier and new or upgraded artillery. The air force ground attack units fly MiG-21s, -23s, SU-25s, and an assortment of other aircraft. Airlift resides in a single regiment that deploys one An-12, three An-24s, four An-26s, 17 assorted L-410s, one Tu-134, and one Tu-154.[47]

The picture of individual national capabilities emerging from the foregoing examination is somewhat cloudy since a number of the states in question have not completed their post–Cold War defense adjustments. Nevertheless, the general outlines and shapes contained in the picture are unmistakable. Every European country scrutinized here is undertaking significant military reductions. Some, including the UK, have reduced their forces significantly. Others are descending into military insignificance.[48] Very few countries have retained the full range of capabilities necessary for unilateral action against a resolute adversary. Most of the European

---

[46]USNI Database *Periscope*, March 1994.

[47]Ibid. See also Czech Republic CFE annual equipment declaration, 15 December 1993, charts I, IIA, IIB.

[48]Field Marshal Sir Peter Inge, Chief of Defense Staff, has expressed fears that with further reductions the British Army would be "on the road to becoming a sort of gendarmerie which can provide a battalion here and a battalion there. . . ." Field Marshal Sir Peter Inge, GCB, "The Capability-Based Army," *RUSI Journal*, June 1994, p. 1.

forces surveyed here are much smaller than the forces they might encounter in Southwest Asia. In some instances, the Europeans would be facing forces with more modern equipment than they possess. One of the potentially most dangerous shortcomings among the Europeans is the lack of theater missile defenses. The Netherlands has purchased Patriot, but otherwise, the Europeans deploy an eclectic mix of air defense systems, most with little or no missile defense capability.[49]

Virtually all of the NATO states surveyed here share a common set of shortcomings. All must rely on commercial transportation to deploy their forces beyond Europe. Some states, such as the French, have developed a sound scheme for doing this—if necessary, they move to an intermediate staging base on commercial carriers and enter the operational area using their tactical and theater transportation. Even so, this mode of deployment is slow and dependent upon finding commercial port facilities to unload the contract ships. None of the allies have an organization capable of opening and operating a port to disembark their forces.

Few countries have the command and control assets necessary to direct large forces. The British, French and Germans are making progress in developing interoperable communications, but most of the allies lack strategic communications. They do not yet have common standards for computers, which are essential to signal interoperability.

Logistics remain tied to home territory. The British are raising two more transport regiments and the French and Germans are developing more mobile support packages for their forces, but for most of the NATO states, their forces remain dependent upon fixed depots or the as-yet slim national support elements in the ARRC, the multinational divisions, and the Eurocorps.

Table 9 compares the forces available for deployment in 1989 before NATO's forces reorganized with those at the end of 1994. Although it

---

[49]It remains to be seen to what extent the defensive umbrella of naval missile defenses can be extended to cover forces ashore. Although the U.S. Aegis system can be employed in this mode, many foreign systems offer only limited terminal defense capabilities.

Table 9

Deployable Military Forces, 1989 and 1994[a]

Country	1989	1994
Belgium	1 Para-commando reg't	Same
Denmark	None	Same
France	FAR (5 divisions), Franco-German bde, Foreign Legion (8500), 1 Marine commando bn	FAR, 1 armor div, Franco-German bde, Foreign Legion
Germany	Franco-German bde elements, 1 anti-tank guided weapon helo reg't	1 armor div, 1 airmobile (ambl) div, 1 avn (helo) bde, 1 support bde
Italy	Rapid Intervention Force (RIF) of 1 abn bde + 4 bns	Same
Netherlands	2 Marine commando groups (2800)	1 ambl bde, 3 Marine bns
Norway	None	Same
Portugal	3 Marines bns, 1 abn bde	Same
Spain	1 ambl bde, Spanish Legion (7000), 1 Marine reg't	1 abn bde, 1 ambl bde, Spanish Legion (6400), 1 Marine reg't
Turkey	1 abn bde, 2 commando (cdo) bde, 1 Marine bde	4 cdo bde, 1 inf reg't, 1 Marine reg't
United Kingdom	3 inf bde, 1 abn bde, 1 inf div, 1 Marine cdo bde	1 armor div, 1 mech+abn div, 1 Marine cdo bde, 1 ambl bde

SOURCES: IISS, *The Military Balance 1989–1990, The Military Balance 1994–1995,* and authors' estimates.

[a]This includes high-readiness units not committed directly to the main defense effort.

is difficult to estimate what units each country might have deployed prior to the end of the Cold War when commitments to the deliberate defense of the Central Region were taken very seriously,[50] it is clear that restructuring the military component of the Alliance has yielded more deployable forces. The French have committed an armored division to the Eurocorps in addition to the forces that they

---

[50]During the Cold War, few forces were not committed to the forward defense. The Allied Command Europe Mobile Force (Land) was a crisis response force, along with its air and naval components. National contributions to the force were small. The United States, for example, committed a single battalion-based airborne task force. Associating other forces with possible crisis response missions requires anticipating how various national capitals would respond to a given crisis.

previously maintained for expeditionary purposes—the FAR and the French component of the Franco-German Brigade. Germany too has increased the size of its crisis response forces. The Netherlands, despite the demands for defense savings, has almost doubled its deployable force structure. Spain and Turkey have also modified their rapid response forces. The British metamorphosis may be the most extensive, with London embarking on the task of providing the "framework" for NATO's Rapid Reaction Corps. The British have completely reorganized their forces for employment in the corps and now provide an armored division and a mixed division that includes both mechanized and airborne forces. Thus, although the military forces of most of the European nations examined here are smaller than they were five years ago, and although the active component of many armies is far smaller than before, Europe has experienced an increase in the forces that its countries could realistically deploy in response to a crisis.

Under budgetary pressures and domestic political imperatives that sought smaller defense establishments, all of the European countries focused their efforts on reducing and restructuring their forces. Virtually all acquisition programs have concentrated on buying weapons systems: new tanks, ships, aircraft, and similar items. There is little evidence that the Europeans have undertaken a review of requirements for munitions and other essential stocks. Some countries, including Germany and the UK, have modernized portions of their munitions—through the RAF acquisition of Paveway III, for example. However, the long-standing reluctance to invest in munitions stocks may be reinforced by today's thinking that crisis management and peace operations will typify future collective military action—activities that are unlikely to make large demands on ammunition and war reserve depots.

Given the very different kinds of equipment and weapons evident in the arsenals of the countries described above, interoperability becomes a major issue. All of the countries surveyed here do not share an agreed approach to doctrine or tactics, or even a common lexicon of military terms. Even for NATO states, logistics remains a national responsibility. In the *ad hoc* world of coalitions of the willing, these interoperability problems could have widely varying consequences depending upon how the coalition forces organize and fight. One approach would be to carry out autonomous but mutually supporting national operations in close proximity to each other. This scheme requires a minimum of coordination among national contingents but virtually no integration of forces. Although this approach to coalition warfare might not have been effective against the Red Army, it might deliver an acceptable level of military effectiveness against Southwest Asian adversaries. A very different approach is to build multinational formations. Depending upon the level to which multinational organization is carried (e.g., corps, division, or brigade), successively more agreement, cooperation, integration, and equipment commonality are required. Experience garnered from NATO, NACC, and PFP will assist the Europeans in determining how to organize coalition operations and how to achieve the required level of interoperability. At present, however, the lack of interoperability looms as a potentially serious impediment to effective, collective military action.

Of course, as the Gulf War demonstrated, the parties to a coalition of the willing are not obliged to provide all of their own war material. Other countries donate ammunition, chemical protective equipment, medical supplies, and even vehicles. Thus, it is conceivable that a multinational organization might overcome some of the military shortcomings of the individual European states by orchestrating and harmonizing the capabilities of participating nations. Chapter Six examines the two most likely candidate organizations, the ARRC and the Eurocorps.

MULTINATIONAL FORMATIONS

Having laid out the essential tasks facing any expeditionary force during an incursion into Southwest Asia and the military capabilities of the principal European states, it remains to determine what multinational formations might serve as the basis for a European collective military response. The probability of a unilateral, national response is minuscule. All of the western European states have embraced multinational formations as the preferred means of carrying out military operations, and many central European states have been quick to see the value of such formations as a pathway to integrating their security with that of western Europe. The most eligible candidate organizations appear to be NATO's ACE Rapid Reaction Corps (ARRC) and the Eurocorps.[1] Smaller formations, including NATO's multinational divisions and the Franco-German Brigade, are not examined individually because they are subordinated to the ARRC and Eurocorps, respectively, and because they are too small to serve as the basis for a European operation in Southwest Asia.

ARRC

Both NATO and the ARRC remain works in progress. The Atlantic Alliance has not finished reshaping itself and refining its role in the greater European security regime. The ARRC is not fully organized,

---

[1]Of course, *ad hoc* formations could be raised as well. This discussion focuses on the ARRC and Eurocorps because they provide concrete examples of multilateral forces and require less speculation than a hypothetical *ad hoc* formation would.

trained, or equipped. The corps emerged from adjustments within the Alliance as its members sought to prepare themselves for the security requirements of the post-Soviet world. As NATO reconfigured its military resources and abandoned the "layer cake" defense along the inter-German boundary, the ARRC was conceived as the principal rapid reaction arm for crisis management and OOTW—activities thought to be likely at and beyond the periphery of Alliance territory. The lack of long-range transport aircraft and modern, high-speed shipping associated with the corps reflects in part historical Alliance neglect, but also suggests that most of the countries providing forces anticipated deploying elements of the corps in and around Europe rather than in more remote theaters.[2]

The ARRC structure allows a building-block process to crisis response. The corps can configure itself for a specific mission by deploying an appropriate mix of forces from the divisions that the member nations have assigned to it. The corps can field airborne, airmobile, armor, mechanized infantry, infantry, mountain, and commando units. The ARRC comprises 10 divisions, but expects never to deploy more than four. Its principal formations are illustrated in Figure 1.[3]

Because it is an Alliance formation, the ARRC would be supported by other NATO assets. It would use the Alliance's AWACS aircraft for airborne early warning and surveillance, and draw combat air support from ACE Mobile Force (Air) squadrons. Standing Naval Force Mediterranean and Standing Naval Force Minesweepers might also augment the corps. Because it is a NATO unit, the corps might have access to U.S. intelligence. If, however, circumstances were to preclude all U.S. support, the ARRC could be aided by other nations with capable intelligence establishments such as Britain and France.

---

[2]The Alliance's new strategic concept seems to support this limited role. See the *NATO Handbook* (Brussels: NATO Office of Information and Press, 1992) pp. 156, 157, especially paragraph 47. See also NATO document MC 317, November 1991.

[3]According to comments by the corps commander, LTG Sir Jeremy Mackenzie, in Peter Saracino, "ARRC at the Sharp End," *International Defense Review*, May 1994, pp. 33–35. Note that the United States participates in the ARRC, but for purposes of this study, the U.S. contingent is not available. In such circumstances, the ARRC would still have nine other divisions from which to choose.

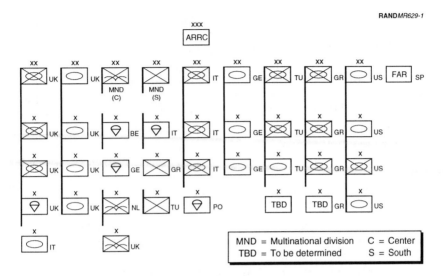

SOURCE: Adapted from Peter Saracino, "ARRC at the Sharp End," *International Defense Review*, May 1994, p. 35.

Figure 1—ACE Rapid Reaction Corps Organization

ARRC's performance in any mission would of course be contingent upon the ability of the contributing nations to perform the minimum, essential tasks confronting them: the ability to maintain peace at home, move significant forces into the region, establish bases, protect the expedition, win the battle, and contain a people's war. Although the corps would have nothing to do with maintaining peace at home, it would be directly engaged in executing the military components of the other essential tasks. The military elements of these tasks include the provision of long-range transportation, intelligence and surveillance, theater missile and air defense, forcible entry, sustainability, and combat power.

Long-range transportation, as noted earlier, remains a problem for the European members of NATO. Nevertheless, innovative steps might mitigate the constraints posed by small military air- and sealift holdings, commercial carriers reluctant to venture into dangerous waters, and the threat of attack submarines, mines, and anti-ship missiles. For example, three nations—Belgium, Norway, and the

Netherlands—have agreed to share their air force transport assets. While these meager holdings would provide only 20 C-130s and 18 assorted transports, the initiative suggests a plan of action that could produce a NATO aircraft pool that might eventually support the ARRC.[4] Several countries are contemplating the purchase of the European Future Large Aircraft (FLA) or the latest version of the Hercules, the C-130J; either aircraft would increase the range to which forces could be projected. Even if the allies fail to buy these aircraft in sufficient quantities to support a massive out-of-area deployment, they might rent AN-124 transports from cash-starved Ukraine, the state that manufactures this aircraft. Kiev would probably be willing to provide the aircraft as a means to earn hard currency and to antagonize Russia by acting against some of her former client states. As an alternative, the Europeans might use the Danube river and European rail network to reach bases in Turkey. This strategy would of course require cooperation from the Balkan and Danubian basin states to allow the European force to transit their territory, as well as that of Turkey—and Turkey's cooperation is no longer a foregone conclusion.[5] Making such arrangements would take a long time.

Historically, the Alliance has relied upon the United States for intelligence and surveillance resources. However, the ARRC could be supported by other, less capable means. With the cooperation of the French, the corps might make use of the Helios, Osiris, and Zenon satellites for surveillance. Commercial satellites might also be employed, including SPOT and LANDSAT. The military value of these systems could be improved by European software vendors who are offering image enhancement packages that can provide one-meter resolution from commercial imagery. NATO's AWACS could be supplemented by less capable British Nimrod systems and by Open Skies monitoring aircraft. Although the sensor suites in certified Open Skies airplanes are based upon 1970s technology, these aircraft

---

[4]See "Belgium, Norway, Netherlands to Share Air Force Assets," *Defense Weekly*, 29 August–4 September 1994, Vol. 9, No. 34, p. 18. In a similar, more recent initiative, France and Britain have discussed creation of a "joint air force" to "undertake a peace keeping role for multinational organizations such as the WEU and the UN." See the U.S. Air Force On-line News Service, 26 October 1994.

[5]See "Turkey may bar strikes from Incerlik base," *Washington Times*, 12 October 1994, p. 14.

would nevertheless provide additional surveillance capabilities. Their utility will improve once the synthetic aperture radars are certified and added to the sensor packages. In addition, surveillance could be improved through the use of drones and unmanned aerial vehicles (UAVs). Many nations have invested in these platforms for tactical surveillance. A pool of CL-289s and similar craft could be deployed to extend the corps' surveillance range. In the absence of JSTARS aircraft, European ASTER might suffice. Finally, the nations supporting the corps all have at least limited human reconnaissance capabilities. Special Air Service, commando, and *Fernspee* units, used in conjunction with the ARRC's Dutch corps reconnaissance troops, should be able to keep the commander well informed about the activities occurring within his area.

Theater missile and air defense pose real dangers for the corps. At present, most NATO members deploy air defense systems that were intended for the integrated air defense of the Central Region. These vestigial systems are aging, but development of replacements has only just begun. A nine-nation European consortium has been formed to develop a new short-range surface-to-air system, but this group will not produce a deployable weapon until early in the next century.[6] Current weapons, such as Hawk, may not be mobile enough to cover the ARRC if they must be hauled in to face the adversary. Missile defense is equally problematic. The corps will have to defend itself against both ballistic and cruise missiles, and at present has only very limited capabilities, principally the Patriot system, to do so. Forces within the envelope of Aegis-equipped ships can be afforded protection, but once they leave the littoral area and move inland, they become vulnerable. France and Germany may participate in the Corps SAM project with the United States, which would produce a very capable missile defense system, but neither has yet reached a decision. As an interim measure, ARRC contributing nations could buy more Patriots or the Russian S-300, a system reputed to be as capable as Patriot.

The current lack of air and missile defenses probably constitutes one of the greatest shortfalls in the ARRC's capabilities. This shortcom-

---

[6]See "NATO Nations Pursue Air Defense System, "*Defense Weekly*, 29 August–4 September 1994, Vol. 9, No. 34, p. 1.

ing could be partially offset with a deterrent strategy. The British could deploy nuclear-capable aircraft as part of the corps' air arm, and prepare one or more ballistic missile submarines for retaliation in the event the ARRC suffers a nuclear attack. This approach, while not addressing all air- and missile-delivered threats, might at least help to manage the risk of a nuclear strike. If nuclear weapons were employed, it would probably change the character of the conflict completely and remove it from the narrow realm of expeditionary military operations considered here.

The ARRC's readiness for forced entry and seizure of bases depends in part upon the location and the circumstances under which it must force its way ashore. Only the French have conducted a forced-entry operation since Suez in 1956, and the French incursion in Zaire was a small-scale operation for which the United States provided the airlift. The British prudently elected to enter the Falklands unopposed and to move over land to the fight. Within the ARRC, there are six brigades of paratroops and a commando brigade that might be used to mount a modest amphibious and parachute assault entry operation. However, the European allies do not have the aircraft necessary to deliver six brigades of paratroops. The assault echelon of a commando brigade might, however, be disembarked from the assortment of LPDs and LPHs in the allied inventory.

Despite the fact that the corps does not seem to have any recent experience or a very credible forced-entry capability, the ARRC has some options on how it might enter the theater that could in part compensate for this operational shortfall. The corps could choose a landing site where it could enter unopposed: within the no-fly zone of Iraq, in a Kurdish-held region, or perhaps on the western shore of Saudi Arabia. NATO might collude with a weak regional state, maybe Jordan, and arrange to base there while allowing the kingdom the deception of resisting allied presence. Another approach might be to align with moderate Arab influences from the Maghreb and enlist an all-Arab force to "liberate" a region that the Europeans could then use as a base.

Of course, there are possible alternative basing modes, depending upon where within the region the crisis unfolds. If the expedition is targeting an adversary in the eastern Mediterranean, the Europeans might base on Cyprus, at least initially. Although far from ideal, such an approach might enable the allies to build up their military capability until they are fully prepared to enter Southwest Asia. This strategy would be akin to the U.S. buildup in Britain during the Second World War before entering Europe on D-Day.[7] Otherwise, the coalition might seek to establish itself in southeastern Turkey or in a remote region within Iraq—perhaps with the Kurdish resistance or in an area over which Baghdad cannot easily exercise its authority, such as the no-fly zone. Another alternative would be sea-basing in the Gulf or Red Sea, presuming that the Europeans could neutralize the Silkworm missiles that might be deployed along the shores. The corps' limited forced-entry capability may not prove to be a serious deficiency in some cases. In some Southwest Asian crises, other NATO forces might already be operating in the region and could host the ARRC. For example, Turkish main defense forces might already be engaged and could facilitate the ARRC's arrival and deployment. The ARRC might be superimposed on the local forces and perhaps serve as NATO's Land Southeast headquarters.

Sustainability for the ARRC depends on the structural readiness of the corps to support its subordinate units, on the stockpiles of munitions and supplies that the nations make available to their divisions within the corps, and on the availability of contract services. Although the structure is not entirely in place, Alliance plans for the ARRC provide typical corps combat service support units adequate for a four-division force. The divisions within the corps that are provided by individual nations each have organic combat support and service support within their structure. Less certain is the support associated with the multinational divisions, where, presumably, the contributing nations will send proportionate support elements with their individual brigades. Also contributing to uncertain adequacy of support is the absence of maritime prepositioned stocks. The United States drew upon six ships based in Diego Garcia for support during the Gulf War. The European allies have none. Most allied nations, in the absence of theater army support elements, will require contracts for commercial support for future operations. At present, NATO regulations restrict contracting to the 16 members, an obvious complication for operations far from Europe. Moreover, the Alliance

---

[7]This, of course, took years, which might render the approach unfeasible for most contingency operations.

has not contracted for services before (it has always been up to the individual nations). If the ARRC or other Alliance formation are to have access to contract-provided support services, either Alliance rules must change and contracting mechanisms established, or procedures must be developed through which participating states coordinate their contract services to economize and prevent duplications of effort.

Within NATO, the size and adequacy of national stockpiles has been a sensitive and contentious matter for years.[8] U.S. and European assessments of what is adequate have differed significantly. Even at the height of the Cold War, many European Alliance members were reluctant to stock the levels of fuel, munitions, and other supplies that the United States thought were necessary for a protracted campaign.

Numbers alone do not cover all of the dimensions of the ammunition issue. Munitions requirements depend to a large degree upon the type of operations that the force undertakes. If the Europeans land unopposed and have time to prepare a deliberate defense, forcing the enemy to come to them to join the battle, the amount of ammunition required might be relatively small. These circumstances would produce relatively heavy requirements for long-range and air-delivered munitions in order to engage the enemy as early as possible. Demand for shorter-range, direct-fire ordnance such as anti-tank guided missiles (ATGMs) and tank main gun ammunition would be proportionately less.

However, if the coalition had to force its way ashore and fight a close-in battle immediately, ammunition requirements could soar, consuming several times the munitions required for a defensive battle. In such a case, shorter-range ammunition would increase in proportionate usage and longer-range munitions would decrease. Many other possible circumstances could influence ammunition requirements. The point is that it is extremely difficult to determine what the size and composition of the ordnance stockpile should be.

---

[8]One need only consider the long-standing practice of some countries in answering the NATO annual defense planning questionnaires, where double counting and circuitous answers are the norm.

The foregoing suggests that ammunition requirements might be quite modest and well within the stock levels maintained by the Europeans. But if the allies find they must conduct a slightly more protracted campaign, or if the air campaign proves less successful, ammunition requirements might grow exponentially. For example, if the same four-heavy-division ARRC were to conduct a five-day-long offensive operation (i.e., only slightly longer than the 100-hour offensive of the Gulf War), the corps might need 265,680 rounds of tank main gun ammunition, 23,512 ATGMs, and over 194,000 rounds of artillery ammunition.[9]

Moreover, while adequacy of munitions is certainly a key factor in the ARRC's ability to prosecute combat operations successfully, it is not the sole determinant of the corps' success. NBC protective clothing, water desalinization and purification capabilities, and similar issues also bear on the problem. Many of the allies are probably lacking in this area, if the British experience in the Gulf War is typical. At the outset of the war, three-fourths of the British army's main battle tanks in Germany (i.e., the bulk of British armor) were under repair. Nor was the army fully ready to protect its forces from NBC attack.[10] France experienced difficulties and shortcomings with its forces in Desert Storm so severe that substantial steps are being taken toward the creation of a more capable intervention force.[11] The crux of the sustainment problem confronting the ARRC and, indeed, any NATO formation is this: during the Cold War, most of the allies deferred buying large stocks for their conventional forces in expectation that any Central European war would quickly escalate to nuclear levels and conventional stocks would be superfluous to the outcome. With the demise of the East-West confrontation and expectation of "peace dividends" in defense reductions, stocks have deteriorated.[12]

---

[9]Authors' calculations using Army estimative techniques derived from U.S. Army Field Manual 101-10-1/2, October, 1987.

[10]Bruce Clark, Bernard Gray, and James Blitz, "UK Forces ill-prepared, says defence report on Gulf War," *London Financial Times*, June 15, 1994, p. 14.

[11]See Christopher Burns, "France undertakes huge buildup in its military forces," *Washington Post*, June 13, 1994, p. 14.

[12]Some modernization has gone on, but gross numbers in war reserve stocks have, for most countries, declined.

The final issue in assessing the ARRC's ability to perform the minimum essential tasks confronting an expeditionary force in Southwest Asia is combat power. Not counting the U.S. contribution to the corps, the ARRC would have at its disposal seven armor brigades, seven mechanized infantry brigades, two airmobile brigades, two infantry brigades, a commando brigade, one mountain brigade, an aviation regiment, and two brigades of types yet to be determined. If the corps commander configured his expeditionary force with heavy divisions, the ARRC would deploy about 1300 tanks, a similar number of ACVs, and some 216 pieces of artillery. Since ACE Mobile Force (Air) has no standing structure but is comprised of whatever squadrons the nations want to contribute, it is difficult to guess what air forces might accompany the corps. At a minimum, the allies would probably deploy a composite wing containing air superiority and ground attack squadrons, as well as tankers and surveillance and support aircraft.

The ground component of this expedition would be relatively small and lacking in artillery, especially multiple launch rocket systems, compared to the notional, eight-division force that an adversary might deploy. If the air forces failed to reduce the enemy significantly, the ARRC might find itself facing an enemy with three times more tanks and armored combat vehicles (ACVs) than the corps could deploy. And the ability of the air forces to do their job would be highly dependent upon securing bases within the region. The allies contributing to the ARRC have little carrier-based air power (e.g., Britain has only three squadrons of Harriers) and similarly limited numbers of tankers able to support operations from more distant bases such as those on Cyprus. Ultimately, the ARRC's combat power depends upon the ability of the corps to gather and organize the other assets discussed above. That is, if the European allies succeed in organizing transportation, intelligence, surveillance, and logistic support in an effective fashion and manage to find modes of operation that minimize the allies' shortcomings, the corps could be a formidable force. The difficulty at present lies in the fact that the ARRC is not fully operational and it is therefore impossible to determine how well the allies are proceeding in each of the critical areas. Figure 2 offers a tentative, overall assessment of the ARRC's suitability for deployment in a major Southwest Asia contingency

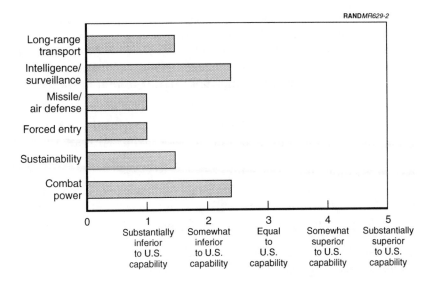

Figure 2—ARRC Military Capabilities Relative to Those of the United States

within the next two years. The figure compares the ARRC to a typical U.S. three-division corps.

The assessment of long-range transportation reflects the lack of military sealift, dependence upon commercial transportation, and paucity of military airlift. Although it is true that the United States made extensive use of commercial airlines and merchant marine vessels during the Gulf War, the United States also presides over a much more capable military transportation fleet. Had the United States been deprived of the use of commercial resources, the nation could still have deployed to the Middle East, albeit in smaller increments, with greater difficulty and over a longer period of time. In contrast, it is clear that no militarily significant portion of the ARRC could be deployed without civil assets, and that the more innovative, alternative approaches to military movement would involve complicated, extended negotiations on rights of transit.

Intelligence and surveillance score somewhat higher because of the expectation that the ARRC could more easily acquire these assets in the absence of U.S. support. The resulting capability would be imperfect; there would be substantial shortfalls in some of the intelligence collection disciplines. The ARRC's surveillance system would have blind spots. Nevertheless, innovative application of existing systems, cooperation among nations to provide satellite coverage, and greater reliance on long-range reconnaissance troops could produce a net capability only somewhat inferior to that of the United States.

The prospects for missile and air defense are more difficult to assess since they depend upon decisions not yet taken. Although the air superiority squadrons of NATO will undoubtedly prove up to their role in warding off enemy fighters, the ground-based accompanying air defenses will be more problematic. Unless a concerted effort is mounted to deal with theater ballistic and cruise missiles, the ARRC will remain vulnerable. Since no program will produce weapons to change these circumstances in the next several years, missile and air defense must be judged to be substantially inferior to those of the United States.

Forced entry, as the foregoing discussion pointed out, can in some circumstances be avoided. Nevertheless, there may be instances that demand it as the only way to get into the theater. The lack of transport aircraft for airborne forces and the modest amphibious capability constitute a serious weakness in the ARRC. The fact that the corps has never practiced such an operation and has never participated in a combined air, sea, and land operation of this magnitude is also a serious shortcoming.

Sustainment has a marginal score because, although the ARRC has begun to develop a support structure to sustain its forces, it has not yet achieved the full capability; it lacks maritime prepositioned ships; it has shortfalls in critical munitions and other war reserve stocks; and procedures for acquiring contract commercial services remain to be developed. Although these deficiencies are a national responsibility for the member nations, collectively they seriously undermine the corps' ability to operate beyond NATO's frontiers.

The combat power at the corps commander's disposal is difficult to evaluate. The ARRC certainly includes a broad mix of forces that afford NATO great flexibility in tailoring a force package. The forces benefit from years of coordination within the Alliance. Many of the member countries deploy the most modern main combat systems—

tanks, artillery, and aircraft. Yet, despite these advantages, several factors detract from the corps' combat power. Most significant among these is the size of the force. A lone corps of four divisions is small when confronting the types of adversaries likely to emerge in Southwest Asia.[13] Even if the ARRC were extremely capable and unimpeded by the shortcomings in capabilities discussed above, it would probably be inadequate if it were the sole instrument of European intervention in the region. Second, although the allies have worked together for years within NATO, this experience has not prepared them for combined arms operations within a single corps. It was a demanding task to harmonize the plans of the corps along the inter-German boundary for deliberate defense of the Central Region. That task pales in comparison to the job of rationalizing the preferred operations practices of divisions from nine different European countries. Finally, the ARRC has not yet fielded the integrated command, control, communications and intelligence system essential to generating combat power.

Based upon these considerations, the ARRC is assessed to be less capable than a U.S. corps. The degree to which the ARRC remains inferior to a comparable U.S. formation may change over time, but until the Europeans find a way to supplement the corps with more forces from the main defense force, Bruce Clark's assessment will remain the case. He wrote:

> [T]he European members of NATO are a long way from possessing the capability to fight even a miniature version of the Gulf conflict on their own. Even if they took a firm decision tomorrow to acquire that capacity as rapidly as possible, they would be hard pressed to do so before the end of the century.[14]

EUROCORPS

Like the ARRC, the Eurocorps is very much a work in progress. The organization has grown around the Franco-German Brigade and has

---

[13]Desert Storm required two U.S. corps and allied and coalition forces constituting the better part of two more corps.

[14]Bruce Clark, "Quarrel in the Family," *London Financial Times*, August 14, 1994, p. 14.

become something of an alternative center for European multilateral military activities. Belgium has recently committed a mechanized brigade to the corps, which will grow to a division by the end of 1995. The Spanish have agreed to provide a mechanized brigade by the end of 1994, and Madrid has also committed itself to supply a 10,000-man division by the end of 1998. Figure 3 summarizes the Eurocorps structure.

The Eurocorps is not entirely independent of NATO or the ARRC. Some of the Eurocorps assets are also committed to NATO—the Belgian division, for example. Moreover, since all of the contributing countries are also NATO members, it may be possible for the Eurocorps to draw on other NATO resources, such as its early warning aircraft or portions of its standing naval forces. Until some coherence in the relations among European security organs appears, it will be difficult to disentangle the Eurocorps from the ARRC and NATO. That said, the corps faces the same problems that affect the ARRC.

Long-range transportation remains a major stumbling block. France, however, offers some capability. Its base in Djibouti provides a toe-hold in the theater that Paris might be able to exploit with

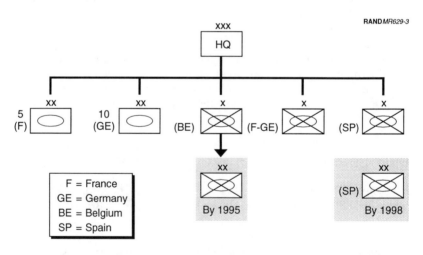

Figure 3—Eurocorps Organization

its two aircraft carriers, five underway support ships, and nine amphibious assault ships. The theater airlift capability centers around four DC-8F, 77 C-160, and 12 C-130 aircraft. Belgium, Germany, and Spain dispose smaller transportation fleets, with Belgium supplying two Boeing 727QC and two HS-748 transports, and about 12 C-130s, while Germany provides roughly 100 aircraft, mostly C-160s. Spain's long-range transportation includes an aircraft carrier and four amphibious assault ships plus a handful of Boeing 707s and C-130s and 32 C-212s. The problem with these resources is that there are too few of them and that very few of the aircraft can deploy tanks and similar heavy weapons, although the Eurocorps is organized around armor and mechanized infantry formations that require large amounts of lift.

As noted above, some capabilities are difficult to evaluate because of the interconnection with NATO assets. That problem holds with intelligence and surveillance. If NATO AWACS and similar resources deploy with the corps, its capabilities should not differ remarkably from those of the ARRC. If Spain and France continue to cooperate on Helios, the military satellite, the Eurocorps may have fair overhead intelligence support.[15] However, as was the case with the ARRC, none of these countries has the same capabilities in all of the intelligence collection disciplines that the United States enjoys. Although France and Belgium in particular deploy modern battlefield surveillance systems and could augment these tools with additional drones and UAVs, they lack certain signals intelligence capabilities.

Missile and air defense prowess will depend in part upon whether or not the Germans and French eventually deploy Corps SAM and modern, short-range air defense systems. If a near-term crisis were to compel the Eurocorps, it could resort to the same quick-fix solutions suggested for the ARRC—purchase or borrow weapons from friends and allies. In addition, the corps might be able to exploit the French tactical and prestrategic nuclear weapons arsenal to discourage nuclear and chemical attacks on the expedition, thus reducing

---

[15]The program is reported to be progressing to the point that the participating states, France, Italy, and Spain, can currently monitor activity in North Africa. See Margaret Bluden, "Insecurity on Europe's Southern Flank," *Survival*, Vol. 36, No. 2, Summer, 1994, p. 138.

the potential for catastrophic losses from air and missile strikes. At present, however, the Eurocorps, much like the ARRC, remains vulnerable in this area.

Forced-entry operations are among the most demanding that any military force can undertake. For a corps comprised mostly of heavy units, such operations may not be possible at all. Unlike the ARRC, which could employ its airborne and airmobile units as an enabling force for a follow-on European contingent, the Eurocorps has no such forces to "hold the door open" for others. Whatever operations the Eurocorps performs, it must perform them with its assigned armor and mechanized units. If the Eurocorps were to deploy alone, it seems doubtful that it could enter the Southwest Asia theater without the assistance of a host nation.

Whether or not the Eurocorps enjoys adequate support depends upon the same two determinants of sufficiency as in the ARRC example: structure and national stock levels. Thus far, the Eurocorps has yet to develop the corps support structure found in the ARRC. Neither corps can be regarded as a mature military organization, but the Eurocorps is less developed than the ARRC insofar as its support structure is concerned. The same logic that influenced stockpile levels among the nations contributing forces to the ARRC manifests itself to some degree among the members of the Eurocorps. The fact remains that most European countries find it increasingly difficult to justify military acquisition programs to their populations.

The Eurocorps' combat power may closely approximate that of the ARRC under some circumstances yet prove to be inferior in other cases. If the adversary chooses to fight conventional engagements, the Europeans, as was the case with the ARRC, would find that they were outnumbered or facing a force of similar size, depending upon how effective the allied air operations were at reducing the enemy forces. The Eurocorps, as a heavy formation comprising four divisions and two mechanized brigades, would be somewhat better off than the four-division ARRC in such a fight, even taking into account the smaller size of the French 5th Armored Division. However, if the enemy were to pursue a people's war strategy, the Eurocorps units would probably prove to be ill-suited for the task. The circumstances then might resemble those that confronted the Soviet military in Afghanistan, where the heavy forces were largely ineffective and

Moscow had to rely on its elite airborne forces and similar units for the bulk of its combat power. The problem for the Eurocorps, should it find itself in similar straits, is that the unit has no such forces—only its heavy divisions and brigades.

Figure 4 offers a summary assessment of the Eurocorps' capabilities relative to those of a U.S. three-division corps, with the same provisos that applied to the assessment of the ARRC: that the unit continues its development and that its ultimate capacity to conduct expeditionary operations may improve. Long-range transportation, missile and air defenses, and sustainability all seem roughly on a par with the capabilities of the ARRC. Transportation into the region is aided somewhat by the French presence in Djibouti and by the assault shipping available to the force. These marginal advantages are offset by the lack of transport aircraft necessary to move the corps' inventory of armored vehicles. Missile and air defenses suffer from the same deficiencies as those of the ARRC. France's nuclear forces may perform a deterrent function to discourage nuclear and biologi-

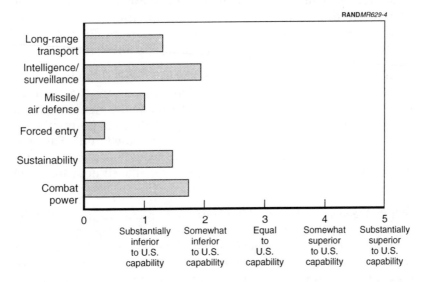

Figure 4—Eurocorps Military Capabilities Relative to Those of the United States

cal attacks on the corps the way British nuclear forces might provide a similar function for the ARRC.

Sustainment for the Eurocorps receives an assessment similar to that for the ARRC because France is modernizing and upgrading its forces, which might have an indirect benefit for the corps, offsetting somewhat any structural deficiencies in the corps' base. Nevertheless, like the ARRC, the Eurocorps lacks maritime prepositioned ships. At present, its ability to sustain itself is considered only marginal.

The Eurocorps appears to be less able than the ARRC in intelligence and surveillance, forced entry, and net combat power. The intelligence and surveillance shortfall may be minimal, but with no British and U.S. participants, the corps will have a more limited view of the battle space and a less comprehensive sense of enemy activities. Perhaps the most profound difference in capabilities is the lack of forced entry. The paucity of long-range transportation and the preponderance of heavy forces in the corps dictate a slow, small-increment deployment. Since such an approach would be inadequate to seize a lodgment in the theater, the Eurocorps will probably not be deployable without the aid of a host nation.

Combat power is assessed as marginally inferior to that found in the ARRC. The heavy-force basis of the Eurocorps means that it has far less flexibility than the ARRC in tailoring itself to the mission at hand. Moreover, although the corps would be well suited (if outnumbered) for an expedition against a conventional foe in the Middle East, that is a less likely event; the more likely enemy would eschew a force-on-force confrontation and seek a people's war–like strategy for which the corps is ill suited.

By themselves, neither the ARRC nor the Eurocorps appears capable of conducting a major combat expeditionary operation in Southwest Asia. The ARRC might provide a light deterrent force if it could deploy early enough, but decisionmaking in NATO is normally a deliberate process, so it seems unlikely that the Alliance could deploy a small force before the situation deteriorated and required a more capable, larger expedition.[16] Neither unit could confront a regional foe alone; both corps are simply too small. Even if no conventional war materialized, neither corps is well suited to contain a people's war. The ARRC might enjoy more success than the Eurocorps because of the types of units that the ARRC could deploy, but both units would find that their small size prevents them from achieving the ratio of troops to population necessary to control a restive people. Assuming each corps deploys around 70,000 personnel, they would achieve a ratio of 7.8:1000 in Syria, 5.5:1000 in Iraq, and 1.8:1000 in Iran— hardly satisfactory if one considers that the British deployed at 20:1000 to control Ulster.

What about employing the two corps together? Conceptually, a force comprised of both corps should be adequate to handle a regional opponent arraying eight divisions. If the European air forces enjoy some success, the expedition's ground forces should face a demoralized, bloodied enemy. Under such circumstances, the coalition should be able to establish favorable force ratios for their main attack of roughly 2.4:1, a margin of advantage deemed acceptable during the Gulf War.[17] Appropriate forces from the ARRC might land first to establish a coalition presence quickly. These units would secure ports and airfields essential to receiving the heavy units. Once a secure lodgment was established, the coalition could bring its logistics ashore and eventually mount combat operations. The key to success for such operations remains speed. If the Europeans cannot deploy quickly to seize and secure a lodgment, they are likely to find that the enemy will have deployed to repulse their landing and to deny them the use of ports and other essential facilities to get ashore.

The Achilles heel of a two-corps operation remains long-range transportation and logistics. If the Europeans would be overtasked to deploy and sustain a single corps as the foregoing examination of their capabilities suggests, then a two-corps expedition would be out of the question. After all, the British had to denude the British Army of the Rhine in order to provide essential equipment and support to the

---

[16]Interviews at AFSOUTH reinforce this point. Even if NATO reaction forces can deploy on 15 days notice (or WEU forces on 30 days notice) the political process is not structured for rapid response. Interview with AFSOUTH POLAD, May 11, 1995.

[17]See Department of Defense, *Conduct of the Persian Gulf War*, Chapter V (Washington, D.C.: U.S. Government Printing Office, April 1992).

two brigades deployed in Desert Storm. If provisioning the divisions of the Eurocorps and ARRC made similar demands on the contributing nations, it would probably strip Europe's main defense forces of essential equipment and supplies. Even if the nations were willing to release the required materiel, they would still not have the means of rapid transport to get their forces to Southwest Asia before a resolute defense could coalesce against them.

What missions remain? The corps might perform limited, punitive expeditions, or provide support to regional governments. Imagine that Iran threatened freedom of navigation in the Red Sea with its Silkworm missiles based in Sudan. The allies could mount an operation based upon the ARRC and Eurocorps units to locate and destroy the missiles. Airmobile elements might embark upon LPHs and move into the Red Sea with appropriate air and naval support. Air and ground reconnaissance would locate the missiles and their hide positions. Where missile batteries could not be easily reconnoitered, the airmobile forces would helicopter into the suspect region and perform a reconnaissance in force. Air and ground forces would destroy the missiles and the allied force would withdraw. The entire operation could be sea based.

Such a mission would be possible because it is not time sensitive, and thus the coalition could prepare for it deliberately, taking the time to select the appropriate units for the operation, moving them to Sudan, isolating the battle space from Sudanese interference, and destroying the Silkworms. Since the force would be confronting Tehran far from its own territory, the prospects of Iran reinforcing or taking other direct military action to confront the operation would be few. The allies could therefore deploy a relatively modest force while still exploiting the command and control and other capabilities of the ARRC headquarters.

Support for a regional government might involve deploying military assistance and training teams, assisting with stability operations against insurgents, or making a show of force to discourage a neighbor from attacking. As noted above, the inability of the multinational formations to respond promptly might be an issue with a show of force, but training and stability operations are well within the capability of these forces. Indeed, French and British units often perform these functions now.[18]

The two multinational corps would seem to have fairly modest capabilities at present. They are not yet fully operational and the nations that provide their forces do not have the long-range transportation and logistics to deploy and sustain these formations at their full four-division strength. As the corps headquarters and corps troops become fully functioning, their capabilities may improve. But until the transportation and logistics shortfalls are addressed, these corps will be limited to deploying far smaller force packages for more limited, less demanding military tasks. Of course, some of the shortcomings noted here would not impede operations within Europe to the same degree. Contingencies at the edge of Eastern Europe could still exploit the European rail network and would also benefit from the dramatically shorter distances involved. But when contemplating operations in remote, distant, austere theaters such as Southwest Asia, the available multinational European corps are clearly deficient.

---

[18]See, for example, Frances Tusa, "France's Forces from the Sea: Interview with Maj. Gen. Tanneguy Le Pichon, Commander of France's 9th DIMA (Marine Infantry Division)," *Armed Forces Journal International* (September 1994), p. 15.

Chapter Seven

CONCLUSIONS

The current European emphasis on out-of-area operations remains largely rhetorical and generally limited to the activities endorsed in the Petersberg Declaration: humanitarian assistance, rescue, and peace operations. It provides some basis for maintaining a few high-readiness units, and its multilateral dimension may mitigate local security fears arising from the military plans of the individual European states. Although some progress has been made preparing multinational European forces for "crisis management" on the periphery of Europe, little has been done to prepare the various military forces for a large combat contingency farther from home. The military establishments of Europe remain oriented toward direct defense of their own territory. Relatively few active duty forces are committed to crisis response and out-of-area activities. Larger proportions of their forces are reservists, while the full-time, regular components have been reduced. Although this arrangement is adequate for direct defense, it makes operations abroad difficult by limiting the forces available for such missions and by depriving them of an adequate rotation base in the event that the undertaking proves to be a long-term one. Furthermore, the emphasis on multinational formations, while forestalling to some degree the renationalization of defense, complicates building coalitions of the willing. For example, if the Europeans wanted to deploy the ARRC but the United Kingdom declined to participate, the corps would be severely handicapped by the absence of its "framework nation" and the headquarters and corps troops that Britain normally provides. The multinational divisions suffer from the same problem.

Even assuming that Europe managed, through some extraordinary feat of will, to assemble an appropriate expeditionary force without the ARRC or the Eurocorps as its basis, the Europeans would still face daunting challenges. The greatest of these problems remains transportation. As Table 10 suggests, the military transport aircraft and ships are few. Access to commercial shipping, as noted above, could vary significantly depending upon the threat to surface carriers, the degree to which insurance companies and nations are willing to indemnify the shipping firms, and the risks that merchant crews are willing to undertake. The European civil air fleet could be similarly discouraged from supporting a dangerous operation, although NATO has organized allied airlift for contingencies and all member nations have some emergency claim on their aircraft.[1] As discussed earlier, the current resources could not deploy and sustain either the ARRC at its full four-division strength or the Eurocorps. Furthermore, recent experience in the region suggests that there would be few participants in a coalition of the willing embarking against a resolute foe.

A related problem for the Europeans involves their war reserve stocks. NATO states have long invested in units and major weapons, presumably for their ability to deter a Cold War enemy, while failing to buy adequate amounts of munitions, medical supplies, fuel, and related expendables essential to the conduct of war, since they expected any conflict would escalate to a nuclear exchange and obviate the need for conventional war materiel. Many nations maintained

Table 10

European Military Transportation

Type	BE	DK	F	GE	GR	IT	NL	NO	PO	SP	TU	UK
Transport aircraft	16	0	93	96	16	52	9	0	28	42	32	97
Transport ships	0	0	15	0	0	0	0	0	0	0	0	0
Large assault ships	0	0	3	0	0	2	0	0	0	3	0	2
Medium assault ships	0	0	5	0	12	3	0	0	0	2	7	6

[1]There are approximately 195 aircraft in the European emergency air fleet as compared with 296 in the U.S. Civilian Reserve Air Fleet. For a description of NATO's civil air organization, see James W. Becker, *European Civil Air: Can NATO Count On It?* (Washington, D.C.: U.S. Government Printing Office, 1989).

only a fraction of the alliance-mandated stockage levels in key munitions and other supplies. Even if ammunition remains adequate to support a short, intense offensive against a Southwest Asian adversary, the expeditionary force could still find itself underprepared for a more protracted struggle that caused it to expend its stocks of NBC protective clothing and equipment, and vehicle and weapons spare parts. Many European armies would find themselves in circumstances similar to those confronting the British in 1990, when the British Army of the Rhine was rendered virtually ineffective after it fully equipped the UK contingent to the Gulf.

If the missile and weapons of mass destruction programs among Southwest Asian nations bear fruit as expected, missile and air defenses will also severely test a European force. Although the full dimensions of the weapons of mass destruction problem certainly are more complex than the contingency force issues dealt with here, unless moderate states in the region acquire appropriate defensive systems the Europeans might have to protect their host nations to retain access to critical facilities. In addition, the expedition would obviously have to protect itself. The present acquisition plans will not produce a viable theater missile defense system in the near term or a fully integrated, high-, medium-, and low-altitude air defense umbrella. As a result, a coalition would be vulnerable to these types of attack and face potentially catastrophic losses if a few nuclear or biological warheads reached the expeditionary force.

Moreover, there is the matter of winning. The Europeans, despite their shortcomings, possess tremendous military skill. So long as they could meet the adversary in a conventional, force-on-force contest without being at a severe numerical disadvantage, the expeditionary force would probably defeat any regional force that could be fielded in the near term. Less certain is the outcome against an asymmetrical strategy or people's war, where the style of warfare might put the Europeans off balance and make them unable to bring their forces to bear effectively. The Europeans would have trouble establishing the presence necessary for effective stability operations in many states of the region because of the size of the indigenous population. In addition, the Europeans lack the rotation base to sustain a role in the theater for an extended period of time.

The danger to Europe could also become a significant determinant of the allies' ability to mount an expedition. The requirement to secure key utilities, cultural artifacts, and similar objects against terrorism or civil unrest could raise demands on the military to augment national police and internal security forces such as the *Gendarmarie* or the *Bundesgrenzschutz*. The prospects of missile attacks and strikes with weapons of mass destruction against European populations could also reduce parliamentary support for an operation in Southwest Asia and strengthen the long-standing tendency of West Europeans to define their security interests in fairly narrow terms of direct and immediate threats to their territory. Ultimately, the confluence of limited capability to project significant military power, political reluctance to engage a determined adversary far from Europe, and fear of the domestic consequences of launching an operation in Southwest Asia may produce multinational military paralysis.

Recommendations

The Europeans could pursue several paths to improve their ability for expeditionary operations. In some instances, they need only reorganize current military assets for more effective employment. In other cases, the Europeans must reach a new consensus on the role of NATO and other regional organizations (e.g., the Organization for Security and Cooperation in Europe, the Western European Union), and the degree to which such organizations' personnel, facilities, and other assets would or would not be available to support coalitions of the willing. In still other instances, the Europeans must first agree that their vital interests are sufficiently threatened by influences beyond their immediate frontiers to warrant spending for additional military capabilities.

Several actions might be included in the first category, actions that could be easily undertaken. The Europeans should organize their existing assault shipping, carriers, and transports to support multinational deployments. The older, less capable large-deck carriers might be converted for duty as CVHs or LPHs to support amphibious operations. The newer small-deck carriers might be specialized in their air wings so that, for example, one might deploy attack aircraft and another air defense and surveillance aircraft. The main point is to coordinate functions among the participants. Even presuming that the expedition is a coalition of the willing in which a number of states decide not to participate, it should still be possible to organize a militarily significant flotilla that might project a modest expedition within the Mediterranean and into the Persian Gulf.

Next, the Europeans should be encouraged to update and expand their air fleets. Current inventories are old and in most instances small. The United States should promote the notion that old airframes should be replaced no less than one-for-one with new, more capable aircraft. In addition, the Europeans would benefit from more tankers to extend the reach of their air transports. Furthermore, the initiative cited above, in which several states have agreed to coordinate the use of their airlift during emergencies, should be promoted Alliancewide. If the Europeans seek a prompt crisis response capability, it can be achieved only by effectively organizing the available aircraft for speedy, coordinated deployment and sustainment of the multinational force.

Since coalitions of the willing seem to be the principal basis for collective military action, each of the European nations should be encouraged to create a strategic command, control, and communications brigade or battalion that will enable its forces to maintain contact with its national leadership, direct its own subordinates, and integrate itself into the communications networks of the ARRC, the Eurocorps, or other *ad hoc* formations. Such a unit could be developed by modifying a current signal battalion and equipping it with appropriate communications suites.

Any expedition venturing abroad will need missile and air defenses. The countries currently contemplating participation in the Corps SAM program should be encouraged to do so. All of the Europeans should be impressed with the need to modernize their accompanying air defense systems. The United States might sponsor a multinational consortium for development and agree to favorable coproduction terms to promote a fully standardized and interoperable system. In addition, the United States might support upgrades to current naval air defense systems such as Sea Dart to give them a limited, anti-missile capability. Alternatively, the United States might make Aegis technology available to European navies.

To the degree that the Europeans can agree on the future role of NATO and its sister regional organizations, the following measures would be useful. NATO must continue to adapt to the new operational requirements. The Alliance's Major NATO Commands (MNCs) lack organic capabilities and cannot contract for commercial support if deployed abroad. Since the Alliance will require commercial contract services to sustain its forces abroad, NATO should build the political authority and contracting procedures to do so. Because major NATO commands are likely to be tasked to direct remote operations, the Alliance should acquire and train a multinational battle staff that is prepared to direct complex operations—not merely to plan them. The United States could make additional billets at the Army's Command and General Staff College and School of Advanced Military Studies available to prepare allied officers for multinational battle staff duties. Most important, perhaps, the Alliance must update its consultative and decisionmaking procedures to enable it to respond promptly to rapidly developing events.

To the degree that the Europeans determine that they must be prepared to protect vital interests beyond their borders and that doing so warrants increased defense spending, two initiatives would be prudent. First, any sizable contingency force requires echelons-above-corps units to sustain it in long-term operations. The NATO of the Cold War era had army groups and fixed depots that provided many of these services to units deployed across the Central Region. For a mobile, expeditionary force, however, these combat support and combat service support capabilities must be organized for deployment. The allies should therefore be encouraged to develop their force structure above the corps and to create a theater army support command that can provide the necessary services and support.

Second, one of the major features that distinguishes the European expeditionary capability described here from U.S. forces is the absence of maritime prepositioned squadrons. These seagoing formations have proved essential to U.S. military deployments by making basic loads of ammunition, essential supplies, medical support, and combat equipment sets available on short notice by positioning them near potential trouble spots. A similar arrangement fielded by the Europeans would reduce the demands on their meager air and sea lift. Prepositioned ships would mean that the Europeans could ship many of their troops by air and use the equipment and supplies on the ships. Such a squadron, located in the eastern Mediterranean or in Djibouti perhaps, could significantly mitigate the strain on European long-range transportation and logistics systems, and thus make the Europeans more capable of independent contingency operations, whether on the immediate periphery of their continent or farther from home. Even a modest squadron of four ships could make a substantial difference—significant enough to warrant spending NATO infrastructure funds to acquire it (and presuming that the details for employment could be worked out to all parties' satisfaction). Furthermore, the equipment set maintained aboard might be made up of tanks and other heavy weapons that would otherwise be reduced under the CFE treaty, providing the squadron were positioned beyond the area of application for the treaty. Costs could thus be minimized. As an alternative to a NATO-owned squadron, Britain might be encouraged to deploy its own to either Oman or Diego Garcia, whereas the French could be encouraged to create such an asset at Djibouti.

More daunting than the difficulties involved in reorganizing the available military resources for an expedition, however, is the matter of generating collective political resolve for concerted military action. As Chapter Four of this report makes clear, an operational paralysis pervades European security. The security architecture remains unfinished, and its overall design is contested by various factional preferences, including those of France, the United States, and the Central and East Europeans. Operations based upon coalitions of the willing reflect in part the widely held notion that many of these missions are elective and without direct influence on the well-being of the majority of Europeans. Until an effective European security regime emerges that can provide commonly held guidelines and mechanisms for collective military action, Europe will remain incapable of prompt and unified military intervention or crisis response.

For its part, in addition to the measures noted above, the United States should exert its leadership to resolve the prevailing strategic paralysis in Europe, help to craft a new consensus on collective military activity, and demonstrate to its European partners that prompt, resolute action can protect mutual interests well beyond the borders of Europe from hostile influences. At a minimum, the United States should:

- Use military-to-military contacts among PFP states to promote a common lexicon of military terms and an agreed set of operational practices. This will provide a minimum degree of interoperability essential for coalition warfare.

- Hold bilateral staff talks with interested states to establish what near-term support their forces would require from the United States in order to participate in a combined expeditionary force. The talks would not necessarily commit the United States to provide the necessary assets, but they would make detailed contingency planning possible and allow the United States and its coalition partners to respond more rapidly in instances when it was mutually beneficial to do so.

- Seek to establish a timetable and force goals with interested states to promote coordinated force development. This initiative would create a partial distribution of labor between the United States and the Europeans to preclude them from spending scarce defense funds on capabilities that the United States could be counted upon to provide.

- Include in the joint five-year exercise schedule combined activities that would require participating European states to plan and execute a brigade-sized deployment using U.S. long-range transportation.

- In instances where a European state is interested in planning assistance, deploy a U.S. joint planning cell to the ministry of defense or appropriate armed forces headquarters to assist in organizing and planning for deployment of the state's expeditionary forces. The planning cell would also provide liaison to appropriate U.S. headquarters involved in deployment of the European state's force.

These rather modest steps could make a substantial contribution toward improving the force projection capability of some European states, coordinating U.S. and European military activities and shoring up the transatlantic relationship. Some critics may complain that the recommendations above give the United States veto power over the military options of other states. That may be true in some instances. But in more circumstances, the United States and some European states are likely to see a mutual benefit in combining their forces to protect a common interest abroad. In those cases, the actions suggested here will promote a prompter, more capable military response.

SELECTED BIBLIOGRAPHY

AK229 DSC/AF (93)2 *North Atlantic Defense and Security Committee 1993 Reports* (October 1993), Sub-Committee on the Future of the Armed Forces Military Trends within the Atlantic Alliance (Brussels: North Atlantic Assembly, 1993).

Becker, James W. *European Civil Air: Can NATO Count On It?* (Washington, D.C.: USGPO, 1989).

"Belgium, Norway, Netherlands to Share Air Force Assets," *Defense Weekly,* 29 August–4 September 1994, Vol. 9, No. 34, p. 18.

Bennett, Bruce W., S. Gardiner, D. B. Fox, and N. K. J. Witney, *Theater Analysis and Modeling in an Era of Uncertainty: The Present and Future of Warfare* (Santa Monica, Calif.: RAND, MR-380-NA, 1994).

Blackwell, James, *Thunder in the Desert: The Strategy and Tactics of the Persian Gulf War* (New York: Bantam Books, 1991).

Bluden, Margaret, "Insecurity on Europe's Southern Flank," *Survival,* Vol. 36, No. 2 (Summer 1994), pp. 138–148.

Borowiec, Andrew, "New NATO intervention force planned for Balkans," *Washington Times,* September 21, 1994, p. 10.

Brauch, Hans Guender, "The New Europe and Non-Offensive Defense Concepts" AFES Press Report No. 15 (Mosbach, Germany, 1991).

Burns, Christopher, "France undertakes huge buildup in its military," *Washington Times,* 13 June 1994, p. 14.

Sharpe, Captain Richard, RN (ed.), *Jane's Fighting Ships 1994–95* (London: Butler and Tanner Ltd., 1994).

Clark, Bruce, Bernard Gray, and James Blitz, "UK forces ill-prepared, says defence report on Gulf War," *London Financial Times*, June 15, 1994, p. 14.

——, "Quarrel in the Family," *London Financial Times*, August 14, 1994, p. 14.

Cooke, James J., *100 Miles from Baghdad: With the French in Desert Storm* (Westport, Conn.: Praeger Publishers, 1993).

Czech Republic, "Information on the Conventional Armaments and Equipment and Personnel Strength of the Armed Forces of the Czech Republic, valid as of January 1, 1994."

de la Billière, Peter, *Storm Command* (London: HarperCollins, 1992).

Department of Defense, *Conduct of the Persian Gulf War* (Washington, D.C.: USGPO, April 1992).

Ehteshami, Anoushiravan, "Iran's National Strategy," *International Defense Review*, April 1994, pp. 29–37.

Feld, Werner J., *The Future of European Security and Defense Policy* (Boulder, Colo.: Lynne Rienner Publishers, 1993).

Fowler, W. W., *Terrorism Database: A Comparison of Missions, Methods and Systems* (Santa Monica, Calif.: RAND, N-1503-RC, 1981).

Freedman, Robert O. (ed.), *The Middle East After Iraq's Invasion of Kuwait* (Gainesville: University Press of Florida, 1994).

Freedman, Lawrence, and Efraim Karsh, *The Gulf Conflict 1990–1991: Diplomacy and War in the New World Order* (Princeton, N.J.: Princeton University Press, 1993).

Gardela, K., and B. R. Hoffman, *RAND Chronology of International Terrorism for 1986* (Santa Monica, Calif.: RAND, R-3890-RC, 1990).

Gazit, Shlomo (ed.), *The Middle East Military Balance 1992-1993*, The Jaffee Center for Strategic Studies (Boulder Colo.: Westview Press, and Tel Aviv: Jerusalem Post, 1993).

Guerin-Sendelbach, Valerie, and Jacek Rulkowski, "'Euro-Trio' Frankreich-Deutschland-Polen," *Aussen Politik*, Jg. 45, 3. Quartal 1994, pp. 246–253.

Heisbourg, François, "France and the Gulf Crisis," in Nicole Gnesotto and John Roper (eds.), *Western Europe and the Gulf* (Paris: The Institute for Security Studies of Western European Union, 1992).

Inge, Field Marshal Sir Peter, GCB, "The Capability Based Army," *RUSI Journal*, Vol. 139, No. 3 (June 1994), pp. 1–5.

International Institute of Strategic Studies, *The Military Balance 1993-1994*, (London: Brassey's, 1993).

Lambert, Andrew, "The Naval War," in John Pimlott and Stephen Badsey (eds.), *The Gulf War Assessed* (New York: Sterling Publishing Co. Inc., 1992).

Lanxade, Admiral Jacques, "French Defense Policy after the White Paper," *RUSI Journal*, April 1994, pp. 17–21.

Lesser, Ian O., *Mediterranean Security: New Perspectives and Implications for U.S. Policy* (Santa Monica, Calif.: RAND, R-4178-AF, 1992).

Maynes, Charles William, "NATO's Tough Choice in Bosnia," *New York Times*, July 27, 1994, p. 21.

McCausland, Jeffrey, *The Gulf Conflict: A Military Analysis*, Adelphi Paper 282 (London: Brassey's, 1993).

McMichael, Scott R., *Stumbling Bear* (New York and London: Brassey's, 1992).

NATO Handbook (Brussels: NATO Office of Information and Press, 1992).

"NATO Nations Pursue Air Defense System," *Defense Weekly*, 29 August–4 September 1994, Vol. 9, No. 34, p. 1.

Operation Granby: An Account of the Gulf Crisis 1990–91 and the British Army's Contribution to the Liberation of Kuwait (London: Ministry of Defence, 1991).

Pagonis, Lieutenant General, William G. with Jeffrey L. Cruikshank, *Moving Mountains: Lessons in Leadership and Logistics from the Gulf War* (Boston: Harvard Business School Press, 1992).

Pimlott, John, and Stephen Badsey (eds.), *The Gulf War Assessed* (New York: Sterling Publishing Co., Inc., 1992).

Republic of Hungary, "Information on the Conventional Armaments and Equipment and Personnel Strength of the Armed Forces of the Republic of Hungary, valid as of January 1, 1994."

Republic of Poland, "Information on the Conventional Armaments and Equipment and Personnel Strength of the Armed Forces of the Republic of Poland, valid as of January 1, 1994."

Rothmell, Andrew, "Iran's Rearmament—How Great a Threat?" *Jane's Intelligence Review*, July 1994, pp. 317–322.

Rühe, Volker, "Perspektiven deutscher Sircherheitspolitik und Zukunftsaufgaben der Bundeswehr," *Europäische Sicherheit*, January 1994, pp. 9–16.

Saracino, Peter (ed.), "ARRC at the Sharp End," *International Defense Review*, May 1994, pp. 33–35.

Sauerwein, Brigitte, "In Transition: The Army of the Czech Republic," *International Defense Review*, April 1994, pp. 69–71.

Schoepflin, George, *Hungary and its Neighbors*, Chaillot Paper #7, Institute for West European Studies, Western European Union, May 1993.

Schulte, Heinz, "Defence chief outlines leaner Bundeswehr," *Jane's Defence Weekly*, September 10, 1994, p. 15.

Slovak Republic, "Information Exchange Pursuant to the Protocol on Notification and Exchange of Information, Army of Slovak Republic, 1st January 1994."

Tusa, Frances, "France's Forces from the Sea: Interview with Maj. Gen. Tanneguy Le Pichon, Commander of France's 9th DIMA," *Armed Forces Journal International,* September 1994, p. 15.

———, "A Not-Very-Bitter Pill: *Armed Forces Journal International,* September 1994, pp. 13, 14.

———, "Kaliningrad Situation Alarming Poles," *Izvestiya,* 9 April 1994, p. 3, as reported in JPRS-TAC-94-004-L, 22 April 1994, p. 14.

U.S. Army Field Manual 101-10-1/2, October 1987.

United States Naval Institute Database *Periscope,* Iraqi Defense Organization/Strength, 15 July 1993.

Watson, Bruce W. (ed.), *Military Lessons of the Gulf War* (Novato, Calif.: Presidio Press, 1991).

Yost, David, "France and the Gulf War of 1990–1991: Political-Military Lessons Learned," *The Journal of Strategic Studies,* 16 (September 1993).